For my wife, Amanda

Thank you for modeling to our children how beautiful it is to pursue God's dreams above our own. May our children grow up to carry your same passion for Jesus to have His inheritance.

"For I will not venture to speak of anything except what Christ has accomplished through me to bring the Gentiles to obedience—by word and deed, by the power of signs and wonders, by the power of the Spirit of God—so that from Jerusalem and all the way around to Illyricum I have fulfilled the ministry of the Gospel of Christ; and **thus I make it my ambition to preach the Gospel, not where Christ has already been named, lest I build on someone else's foundation**, but as it is written, 'those who have never been told of Him will see, and those who have never heard will understand.'"

Romans 15:18–21

CONTENTS

PREFACE 9

INTRODUCTION 11

SECTION 1
THE SIMPLICITY OF DISCIPLE-MAKING 15

SECTION 2
THE URGENCY OF DISCIPLE-MAKING 51

SECTION 3
THE JOY OF DISCIPLE-MAKING 75

CONCLUSION 101

APPENDIX A
COMPEL THEM TO COME IN 101

APPENDIX B
A FULL GOSPEL WITNESS 121

APPENDIX C
THE GRACE WHICH SAVES 127

ACKNOWLEDGMENTS 131

ABOUT THE AUTHOR 133

ABOUT FAI 133

PREFACE

I really like the parable of the wedding feast. It has to be my favorite parable, by far. In many ways, it has shaped the way I live and has given structure to the way I witness to the lost.

The King sent servants along highways and hedges to compel as many people as they could find to come to the wedding feast. This included homeless, lame, and blind people. Colorado Springs is home to many people living in the streets. As my wife and I prepared for our 2015 wedding there, we often thought about this parable and even considered inviting a homeless person to our wedding.

After our wedding ceremony, as we walked down the street toward the reception venue, Amanda was complimented on her dress by a homeless woman at a bus stop. I whispered into my wife's ear and, nodding in agreement, she turned to the woman and asked her to join us at the wedding reception. That night the homeless woman enjoyed good food, fun music, and friendly company at our wedding feast. She had a great time, and was very thankful. That woman would never have dreamt of attending our wedding reception if my wife and I had not invited her in. In fact, she wouldn't even have known about it. Our wedding reception served as such a real insight into the task we've been given as Christians to invite men and women to the ultimate wedding banquet in the age to come: the Marriage Supper of the Lamb! Truly:

"Blessed are those who are invited to the marriage supper of the Lamb."[1]

1 Revelation 19:9

INTRODUCTION

The parable of the wedding feast is unique. While it tells us what the Kingdom of God is like, it also describes in part what the Kingdom of God actually is. Most parables are stories that convey meaning through comparison or analogy, but this particular parable is more than that. The imagery used here accurately describes the Christian enterprise in terms that carry significance, both in this age and in the age to come.

Yes, the Kingdom of God may be compared to a king who put on a wedding banquet for his son. But it also describes who God is and what he's actually doing. He really is the king. God really has a Son. There will really be a marriage feast when He returns. We really are servants of the master. We really have been commissioned to invite men and women to be reconciled to Him so that he may enjoy them forever.

I've layered together excerpts from both Luke's and Matthew's accounts of this parable to emphasize specific points that especially inspire action. I'll refer to these passages throughout the book.

> "And again, Jesus spoke to them in parables, saying, 'The Kingdom of Heaven may be compared to a king who gave a wedding feast for his son and sent his servants to call those who were invited to the wedding feast, but they would not come. Again, he sent other servants, saying, "Tell those who are invited, "'See, I have prepared my dinner, my oxen

and my fat calves have been slaughtered, and everything is ready. Come to the wedding feast.'" But they paid no attention and went off."[1]

"But they all alike began to make excuses."[2]

"So, the servant came and reported these things to his master. Then the master of the house became angry and said to his servant, 'Go out quickly to the streets and lanes of the city, and bring in the poor and crippled and blind and lame.'"[3]

"Invite to the wedding feast as many as you find."[4]

"And the servant said, 'Sir, what you commanded has been done, and still there is room.' And the master said to the servant, 'Go out to the highways and hedges and compel people to come in, that my house may be filled.'"[5]

"So, the wedding hall was filled with guests. But when the king came in to look at the guests, he saw there a man who had no wedding garment. And he said to him, 'Friend, how did you get in here without a wedding garment?' And he was speechless. Then the king said to the attendants, 'Bind him hand and foot and cast him into the outer darkness. In that place, there will be weeping and gnashing of teeth.' For many are called, but few are chosen."[6]

The guests in this parable are not only attendees and observers, but they and the servants are also future members of the body of Christ who are being gathered together into God's kingdom! God wants His house to be filled with those to "whom He has given the right to become children of God."[7] And He wants us to go out and bring them in.

---

1 Matthew 22:1-5
2 Luke 14:18a
3 Luke 14:21
4 Matthew 22:9
5 Luke 14:22-23
6 Matthew 22:10-14
7 John 1:12-13

It's essential to take note that the master sent his servants to invite poor and lame people to a wedding, and then becomes furious with those who show up without proper wedding attire. But why? How can He be angry with a homeless person for not having a tuxedo?

The wedding garment Jesus spoke of in this parable is referring to the garments of salvation spoken of by the prophet Isaiah:

> *"He has clothed me with the garments of salvation;*
> *He has covered me with the robe of righteousness."*[8]

The master is right to be angry with guests who show up without proper wedding attire because he is handing out free garments of salvation at the door. Jesus used this parable to rebuke the pharisees for rejecting him as messiah. He's telling them that they cannot enter the kingdom of heaven by their own righteousness, but that they must accept the free gift of Jesus' righteousness.

While it's vital that we understand this parable in the context Jesus gave it in, I think it's helpful and does no harm to consider also how the imagery used here depicts what the Lord is actually doing in our day to bring salvation to the lost.

The following chapters of this book will follow the flow of this parable to help us explore the simplicity of the Christian responsibility as servants, the urgent nature of the task we've been given, and the joy of bringing people to the Lord—so that His house may be filled with guests. As servants of Jesus, whatever our perceived personal callings may be, we first have a call to make disciples; a call to help announce the good news of God. We have *a call to compel*.

I pray this book would help produce an earnest desire to answer that call. It's my way of saying, "Magnify the LORD with me, and let us exalt His name together!"[9]

---

8   Isaiah 61:10
9   Psalm 34:3

SECTION I

THE SIMPLICITY OF MAKING DISCIPLES

"[The master] sent his servants to call those who were invited to the wedding feast, but they would not come."[1]

If you are a Christian, you have been approved by God to be entrusted with the Gospel. You are a servant of Christ and a steward of the good news of God.

> "This is how one should regard us, as servants of Christ and stewards of the mysteries of God....Moreover, it is required of stewards that they be found faithful."[2]

> "For our appeal does not spring from error or impurity or any attempt to deceive, but just as we have been approved by God to be entrusted with the Gospel, so we speak, not to please man, but to please God who tests our hearts."[3]

We have been approved. We have been entrusted. Let's be found faithful.

---
1   Matthew 22:3
2   1 Cotinthians 4:1-2
3   1 Thessalonians 2:3-4

When Jesus called His disciples, He urged them to two things, "That they might be with Him and that He might send them out to preach."[4] If there is a special calling to share the Gospel, salvation itself is that calling. If a qualification is necessary, simply being with Jesus qualifies us to share His good news with the lost.[5]

The early disciples understood the calling of every believer to steward the good news entrusted to them, regardless of their vocation. We are all held responsible to "make disciples"[6] wherever we live and go; this command is often much simpler than we have led ourselves to believe. We'll explore that in this section.

Stephen, from the book of Acts, was not an apostle or evangelist, but he was stoned to death for preaching the Gospel.[7] Stephen had a good reputation and was full of the Spirit, but his primary job was to serve tables so that others could devote themselves full-time to the preaching of God's Word.[8] He was a layman with a service job. Yet he understood that, as a believer, vocations are subservient to obeying Jesus' commission to tell others the good news. Imagine what it would be like if every Christian took responsibility for announcing the Gospel in the way that Stephen and the early disciples did. How many nations would we still be referring to as "unreached" or "unengaged"?

When it comes to sharing the Gospel, it can be tempting to believe that the responsibility lies primarily on the evangelist or paid church staff. According to Paul, the evangelist's role (alongside apostles, prophets, teachers, and shepherds) is to equip laypeople for the work of ministry.[9] It's a service role, to build up and encourage believers in the knowledge of the Son of God until we are all confident in sharing the good news with others. Laypeople are the actual workforce; evangelists are simply their servants for the cause.

Think of an evangelist as you think of a worship leader. Both are servants of the congregation to help equip and lead, respectively. We would never expect worship to be done by the worship leader alone

---

4   Mark 3:13-14
5   Acts 4:13
6   Matthew 28:19-20
7   See Acts 7
8   Acts 6:2-5
9   Ephesians 4:11-12

while we sat back and observed. In the same way, we shouldn't expect evangelism to be done by evangelists alone. Not everyone needs to become an evangelist. But we should all be moving toward greater ownership of our responsibility to God and to the lost people around us. Whatever our vocation, we are servants first—and we are spouses, parents, students, baristas, educators, first responders, city workers, *insert-your-life-here* second. And servants get sent out to gather the lost.

There is a simplicity that comes with understanding our identity as a servant of God: He is the Master. We are the servants. We have been sent out to compel to come in as many people as we can find. There's really not much more to our role than that. It was said of the disciples, Peter and John, that though they were uneducated, common men, people were astonished at their boldness, recognizing that they had been with Jesus.[10] The simplicity of belonging to Jesus is what authorizes us to be His representatives.

> "For consider your calling, brothers: not many of you were wise according to worldly standards, not many were powerful, not many were of noble birth. But God chose what is foolish in the world to shame the wise; God chose what is weak in the world to shame the strong; God chose what is low and despised in the world, even things that are not, to bring to nothing the things that are, so that no human may boast in the presence of God."[11]

There are no academic requirements to be a servant sent by God. Someone who is academically inclined is just as indispensable to the kingdom as someone who is not. All people can be used by the Lord if we approach the mysteries of God with humility and childlike wonder.

> "At that time Jesus declared, 'I thank You, Father, Lord of heaven and earth, that You have hidden these things from the wise and understanding and revealed them to little children.'"[12]

The good news of God is simple. Even children can understand the

---
10   Acts 4:13
11   1 Corinthians 1:26-29
12   Matthew 11:25

Gospel when it is presented to them appropriately. It doesn't have to be complicated. Emphasizing the simplicity of the Gospel message can help remove discouragement and feelings of inadequacy that would prevent us from sharing this excellent news. When we have *clarity* on the message, we have *confidence* in proclaiming it.

THE ELEMENTARY GOSPEL

Most of us are probably familiar with this verse in Romans: "For everyone who calls on the name of the Lord will be saved. How then will they call on Him in whom they have not believed? And how are they to believe in Him of whom they have never heard? And how are they to hear without someone preaching?"[13]

In light of this verse, I think it's helpful to question what is necessary for a lost person to understand to call on the name of the Lord for salvation. I believe every clear and biblical articulation of the Gospel must include that man has inherited a corrupted nature and will be judged eternally; that Jesus is the Son God, born of a virgin and without sin; that God rescued man from wrath by punishing His innocent Son in their place; that Jesus was resurrected from the dead and ascended into Heaven until His return; and that every person hearing the good news is accountable and responsible for repenting from sin and turning toward Christ. (For a more detailed account of the Gospel as delivered by the prophets and apostles, including Scripture references, please see Appendix B.)

But is that all it takes for a person to be convinced of their need for salvation? Or is there something in addition to sound preaching that must be understood and applied? While theological accuracy is imperative, it may not be our precise articulation alone that proves most compelling to the lost people we're aiming to reach. As we survey the good news of God, it's essential to keep in mind that accurate content by itself may not sufficiently compel a person to call on the Lord for salvation. There may actually be more we can do for them.

CONTEXT

Understanding the truths about God and man, while simple, can be overwhelming to those who don't have a history with the information. Context is important. Peter's first sermon was readily accepted

---

[13] Romans 10:13-14

because his audience had a prophetic framework. Jews were familiar with the Law and the Prophets and had been taught to expect the coming Messiah. Introducing Jesus from Nazareth as the awaited Messiah could make sense to them because they had been taught to expect Him from an early age. Peter could come out of the proverbial preaching gate with a sermon like this:

> "Brothers, I may say to you with confidence about the patriarch David that he both died and was buried, and his tomb is with us to this day. Being, therefore, a prophet, and knowing that God had sworn with an oath to him that he would set one of his descendants on his throne, he foresaw and spoke about the resurrection of the Christ, that he was not abandoned to Hades, nor did his flesh see corruption. This Jesus God raised up, and of that, we all are witnesses."[14]

But for those who don't have this context, it can take some time to process. No matter how clear we are, many people would have just heard a whole lot of new information that they may not be able to retain, much less understand and obey. So, we may need to consider that communicating this content all at once might not be the most effective way for them to learn it. It may be for some, but we should be careful not to build our evangelistic efforts around a single approach. One size may not fit all.

We need to avoid the mistake of operating with an approach that assumes someone hearing the Gospel will be able to retain it, understand it, and weigh the new knowledge against their previously held belief system in a matter of minutes. How will it serve a Muslim if we expect them to make a life-altering decision by giving their allegiance to the Son of God just a few minutes after you told them the good news for the first time? That's a lot to do in a short time. Perhaps we should employ an approach that instead encourages long-term engagement and relationship with those who receive the Gospel message from us.

The majority of the world's population doesn't understand the Law of Moses. Most Muslims and Buddhists are not familiar with Jewish

---

[14] Acts 2:29-32

prophecies concerning the Messiah. Articulating facts about sin and the sacrifice of Jesus may be enough for those in reached Western cultures and communities, because these people groups usually have enough as a colloquial reference point. For others, starting with the cross may neglect volumes of invaluable revelation that can help build the context where Jesus as Messiah actually makes sense to them.

As ideal as it would be, the ordinary course of human life doesn't often provide adequate time to sufficiently exhaust all of our evangelistic efforts in just one meeting with a stranger. This is why I believe it may require a change in our thinking. We can no longer think of preaching the Gospel exclusively as a one-off, well-polished, five-point sermon to be given and either accepted or rejected on the spot. It can be that for some, but we must think of our preaching as one necessary component in an ongoing relationship with those we are discipling, even before they are saved.

THE GOOD NEWS OF GOD

As we consider our role as servants—as disciples who make disciples—it's crucial that we have clarity on the whole message we are expected to deliver. One of the wonders of God displaying His glory in the face of His Son is how He revealed to the prophets everything that would unfold before it happened.[15] The descendants of Adam always knew there would be One to crush the head of the serpent because God promised He would send one.[16] The Jewish people knew this Messiah would come through the lineage of Abraham,[17] be born of a virgin in Bethlehem,[18] and rule in Israel[19] from the throne of His father David forever.[20] They knew this because the prophets told them beforehand.

So, what should we do for people who do not know these things already? How do we serve the lost who have no context for a promised Messiah? We need to actively and prayerfully position ourselves in the lives of people around us. We need begin intentional relationships with the lost and disciple them toward Jesus. We need to come alongside them, day-in and day-out, and bring them on a journey of

---

15   Amos 3:7
16   Genesis 3:15
17   Genesis 12:3
18   Isaiah 7:14
19   Micah 5:2
20   2 Samuel 7:16

discovering God through reading, obeying, and sharing the Bible. It's incredible how many unbelievers will walk this journey with you, long before they are even saved. God is working on people. He is drawing them toward His Son. And we *get* to be a part of that.

While bringing these unbelievers on the journey, we can give them the context in which Jesus as Messiah makes sense to them. We can help them see the problem of mankind's sin and the necessity for salvation. We can help them understand the expectancy the Jewish people had for centuries that the Messiah would come to them. When they understand the prophetic framework they will be all the more excited when they see that Jesus has so far fulfilled every prophecy concerning Himself precisely as the Bible predicted He would. And this will give them hope that He will continue to fulfill all of the promises still outstanding.

> *"For I delivered to you as of first importance what I also received: that Christ died for our sins in accordance with the Scriptures, that He was buried, that He was raised on the third day in accordance with the Scriptures."*[21]

To Paul, it was of utmost significance that the events of Jesus' life were predicted long before they happened and were fulfilled exactly as the prophets had written them. It tested the authenticity of Jesus' claim to be the Son of God. Without proven, fulfilled prophesies from the past, it would be unnecessarily difficult to ask someone to believe that the future prophecies of God will come to pass. But with them, it will be much harder to deny. We can serve the lost people in our context by offering them a firsthand look at the biblical accounts where God had begun foreshadowing His Son. This will take time. It's a long road to have a relationship with a person and facilitate them discovering God in the face of Jesus. It took the Lord over 2,000 years from the time of His promise to Abraham to send to Jesus to Earth. It will likely take us more than twenty minutes. Discipleship requires a relationship.

After Jesus resurrected from the dead, He was walking on a road and began talking with two men on their way to a village named Emmaus. As they spoke, Luke records, "And beginning with Moses

---
21 1 Corinthians 15:3-4

and all the prophets, He interpreted to them in all the Scriptures the things concerning Himself."[22] John records Jesus saying, *"For if you believed Moses, you would believe Me; for he wrote of Me."*[23]

For those who have eyes to see, this is one of the most exhilarating passages in the Bible. Jesus, in resurrected flesh, personally shared the good news with these men by pointing to the Scriptures that were ultimately pointing to Himself. What an incredible privilege it would have been to hear the Gospel directly from Jesus' mouth. Jesus left us a good road map to follow as we bear witness to the lost. He didn't start with the events that had happened during that pivotal week. He didn't begin by explaining substitutionary atonement. Jesus began with Moses and the Prophets. He started in the beginning.

To help me remember the crucial components of the Gospel, I like to outline the story with 7 Cs: Creation, Consequences, Covenants, Commands, Christ, Crucifixion, and Coming. Others may have a different approach for remembering the whole story, and that's great too. Use whatever works best for you.

CREATION

In the beginning, God created the heavens and the earth.[24] What distinguishes this account of creation from the way other religions tell it is the fact that Jesus was present during this miraculous occasion. It's crucial that the lost people we're discipling recognize this distinction. That doesn't have to happen the first time you meet together, but at some point, in their discipleship they will need to embrace this reality. Many people we share with will likely come from other cultures and backgrounds that hold very warped versions of this story.

> "In the beginning was the Word, and the Word was with God, and the Word was God. He was in the beginning with God. All things were made through Him, and without Him was not anything made that was made…and the Word became flesh and dwelt among us, and we have seen His glory, glory as of the only Son from the Father, full of grace and truth. (John bore witness about Him, and cried out,

---

22 Luke 24:27
23 John 5:46
24 Genesis 1:1

"This was He of whom I said, 'He who comes after me ranks before me because He was before me.'")[25]

"He is the image of the invisible God, the firstborn of all creation. For by Him, all things were created, in heaven and on earth, visible and invisible, whether thrones or dominions or rulers or authorities—all things were created through Him and for Him. And He is before all things, and in Him, all things hold together. And He is the head of the body, the church. He is the beginning, the firstborn from the dead, that in everything He might be preeminent. For in Him, all the fullness of God was pleased to dwell."[26]

CONSEQUENCES

The Bible is full of implications for those who set themselves against their loving Creator. When Adam and Eve are deceived by the serpent to disobey God, He casts them out of the garden.[27] But one of the remarkable things about God's consequences is that He often provides a way of redemption. Though God removed the couple from the Garden, He made them a promise, that from their offspring He would give a Son to crush the head of the lying serpent.[28] They were expelled from the Garden to prohibit their access to the Tree of Life in a way that would perpetuate their dying condition.[29]

In Noah's day, when the entire world had abandoned their Maker, the Lord was grieved and decided to blot out men whom He created. Noah found favor in God's eyes and his family was spared. During the years Noah built the ark, he heralded righteousness to the people. If anyone got on the ark with Noah's family, they would have survived God's wrath. It's helpful for our unbelieving friends and colleagues to recognize this. When they begin to understand the severity of the consequences they deserve for sinning against God, they will already have a reference point for God as a refuge for those who will hide in His Son.

25　John 1:1-3,14-15
26　Colossians 1:15-19
27　Genesis 3:22-24
28　Genesis 3:14-15
29　Genesis 3:22-24

"The Lord saw that the wickedness of man was great in the earth and that every intention of the thoughts of his heart was only evil continually. And the Lord regretted that He had made man on the earth, and it grieved Him to His heart. So, the Lord said, 'I will blot out man whom I have created from the face of the land, man and animals and creeping things and birds of the heavens, for I am sorry that I have made them.' But Noah found favor in the eyes of the Lord."[30]

Covenants

God made covenantal promises to Abraham, the descendant of Eve. The Lord called Abraham (at that time, Abram) out of his home and promised to make his offspring a great nation in specific land and that they would bless all the families of the earth.[31] At the time God promised these things to Abraham, he was childless, and his wife was barren.[32] Nevertheless, God promised to make his offspring as innumerable as the starts. The Lord caused a deep sleep to come over Abraham so that God alone entered into a one-way, unconditional, everlasting covenant to give him land, offspring, and blessing.[33]

> "And I will give to you and to your offspring after you the land of your sojourning, all the land of Canaan, for an everlasting possession, and I will be their God."[34]

It's vital that we know what was promised to Abraham because this is one of the weightiest and consequential promises made in the Bible. And it's essential that we know Abraham was asleep for it, because it shows more convincingly the unchangeable nature of God's character to the heirs of the promise. It shows that no matter what Abraham or his children after him do or don't do, God will keep His Word!

> "For when God made a promise to Abraham since He had no one greater by whom to swear, He swore by Himself, saying, 'Surely I will bless you and multiply

---
30   Genesis 6:5-8
31   Genesis 12:1-3
32   Genesis 11:30; Romans 4:19
33   Genesis 15:1-21
34   Genesis 17:8

you.' And thus, Abraham, having patiently waited, obtained the promise. For people swear by something greater than themselves, and in all their disputes, an oath is final for confirmation. So, when God desired to show more convincingly to the heirs of the promise the unchangeable character of His purpose, He guaranteed it with an oath, so that by two unchangeable things, in which it is impossible for God to lie, we who have fled for refuge might have strong encouragement to hold fast to the hope set before us. We have this as a sure and steadfast anchor of the soul, a hope that enters into the inner place behind the curtain, where Jesus has gone as a forerunner on our behalf, having become a high priest forever after the order of Melchizedek."[1]

God promised the Jewish people that He will not by any means or for any reason, break His covenant with Abraham. He says that so they might have strong encouragement to hold fast to the hope set before them.

COMMANDS

The Lord gave Israel the commandments of the Law so they might stay long in the Land He promised them.[2] But He warned them that if they act corruptly, they would be temporarily removed from the Land.[3] The law was for discipline, because the Lord disciplines every son whom He loves.[4] But the Lord made it very clear, that whether Israel dwells long in the land or is temporarily removed because of their corruption, that He will cause them to return in the last days to keep His promise to Abraham.

> "When you are in tribulation, and all these things come upon you in the latter days, you will return to the Lord your God and obey His voice. For the Lord, your God is a merciful God. He will not leave you or destroy you or

---

1 Hebrews 6:13-20
2 Deuteronomy 4:1-2
3 Deuteronomy 4:25-27
4 Proverbs 3:11-12

forget the covenant with your fathers that He swore to them."[5]

The Law served as a guardian and manager until the fullness of time, when Jesus would come and redeem those who were under its care—to adopt them as sons.

> "I mean that the heir, as long as he is a child, is no different from a slave, though he is the owner of everything he is under guardians and managers until the date set by his father. In the same way, we also, when we were children, were enslaved to the elementary principles of the world. But when the fullness of time had come, God sent forth His Son, born of woman, born under the law, to redeem those who were under the law, so that we might receive adoption as sons."[6]

Paul explains how the law helps make humans accountable to God through the knowledge of sin. The law makes us excuse-less before God.

> "Now we know that whatever the law says it speaks to those who are under the law, so that every mouth may be stopped, and the whole world may be held accountable to God. For by works of the law, no human being will be justified in His sight, since through the law comes knowledge of sin."[7]

The law is essential for proving Jesus' sinlessness. If there was no law, and morality was arbitrary, how would we have been able to judge Jesus' moral perfection? It's essential that our unbelieving friends and family recognize the sinlessness of Jesus. We know from the law that only a lamb without blemish or spot is acceptable to God.[8] Jesus is the spotless Lamb who takes away the sins of the world.[9]

> "You were ransomed from the futile ways inherited from

---

5   Deuteronomy 4:30-31
6   Galatians 4:1-5
7   Romans 3:19-20
8   Exodus 12:5
9   1 John 1:29

your forefathers, not with perishable things such as silver or gold, but with the precious blood of Christ, like that of a lamb without blemish or spot. He was foreknown before the foundation of the world but was made manifest in the last times for the sake of you who through Him are believers in God, who raised Him from the dead and gave Him glory, so that your faith and hope are in God."[10]

"He made Him who knew no sin to be sin on our behalf so that we might become the righteousness of God in Him."[11]

CHRIST

God made a promise to King David, the descendant of Abraham, that his Son would build a house for God and would rule over Israel forever. "When your days are fulfilled, and you lie down with your fathers, I will raise up your offspring after you, who shall come from your body, and I will establish His kingdom. He shall build a house for my name, and I will establish the throne of His kingdom forever."[12]

As with His covenant with Abraham, the Lord alone makes this one-way, unconditional promise to David and his offspring. In other words, nothing can stop this from happening the way God said it will happen.

The book of Matthew opens with this line: "The book of the genealogy of Jesus Christ, the son of David, the son of Abraham."[13] Jesus is the Son promised to David to rule on his throne forever. Jesus is the One who will ensure that God's covenant with Abraham will be exacted. Jesus is the Son God promised to Eve so long ago in the garden. He is the one who inaugurated the New Covenant with the house of Israel by the shedding of His blood.[14] He is the long-awaited Jewish Messiah.

CRUCIFIXION

God promises Israel salvation through the crushing His own Son for their sins.

---

10 1 Peter 1:18-21
11 2 Corinthians 5:21, NASB
12 2 Samuel 7:12-13
13 Matthew 1:1
14 Isaiah 59:20-21l Jeremiah 31:31-34; 32:37-42; Ezekiel 36:22-28; 1 Corinthians 11:25

"Surely, He has borne our griefs and carried our sorrows; yet we esteemed Him stricken, smitten by God, and afflicted. But He was pierced for our transgressions; He was crushed for our iniquities; upon Him was the chastisement that brought us peace, and with His wounds, we are healed. All we like sheep have gone astray; we have turned—every one—to his own way; and the Lord has laid on Him the iniquity of us all. He was oppressed, and He was afflicted, yet He opened not His mouth; like a lamb that is led to the slaughter, and like a sheep that before its shearers is silent, so He opened not His mouth. By oppression and judgment, He was taken away; and as for His generation, who considered that He was cut off out of the land of the living, stricken for the transgression of my people? And they made His grave with the wicked and with a rich man in His death, although He had done no violence, and there was no deceit in His mouth. Yet it was the will of the Lord to crush Him; He has put Him to grief; when His soul makes an offering for guilt, He shall see His offspring; He shall prolong His days; the will of the Lord shall prosper in His hand. Out of the anguish of His soul, He shall see and be satisfied; by His knowledge shall the righteous one, My Servant, make many to be accounted righteous, and He shall bear their iniquities. Therefore, I will divide Him a portion with the many, and He shall divide the spoil with the strong because He poured out His soul to death and was numbered with the transgressors; yet He bore the sin of many, and makes intercession for the transgressors."[15]

Jesus was crucified for the sins of the world. He died and was buried and resurrected from the dead. He then appeared to over 500 men before ascending to the right hand of the Father.[16] There are over 500 eyewitnesses to the crucifixion and resurrection of Jesus. This too is very significant for our unbelieving disciples to recognize. Especially those from a Muslim background, who are taught from birth that Jesus is not God, that He was not crucified, and that He did not

---

15 Isaiah 53:4-12
16 Acts 1:9-11; 1 Corinthians 15:3-6

resurrect from the dead. Everything hinges on His death and resurrection. Paul knew this well:

> "And if Christ has not been raised, then our preaching is in vain, and your faith is in vain...If in Christ we have hope in this life only, we are of all people most to be pitied."[17]

Coming

Jesus Christ is coming back, and He's bringing His Kingdom with Him!

He is coming back to keep every promise God has made to mankind. We'll survey several of them here. To begin, it may surprise us to find these promises include and require He return to judge and to make war:

> "Then I saw heaven opened, and behold, a white horse! The One sitting on it is called Faithful and True, and in righteousness, He judges and makes war."[18]

> "Behold, a day is coming for the Lord when the spoil taken from you will be divided in your midst. For I will gather all the nations against Jerusalem to battle, and the city shall be taken and the houses plundered and the women raped. Half of the city shall go out into exile, but the rest of the people shall not be cut off from the city. Then the Lord will go out and fight against those nations as when he fights on a day of battle. On that day His feet shall stand on the Mount of Olives that lies before Jerusalem on the east, and the Mount of Olives shall be split in two from east to west by a very wide valley so that one half of the Mount shall move northward, and the other half southward."[19]

> "They will make war on the Lamb, and the Lamb will conquer them, for He is Lord of lords and King of kings, and those with Him are called and chosen and faithful."[20]

---

17   1 Corinthians 15:14,19
18   Revelation 19:11
19   Zechariah 14:1-4
20   Revelation 17:14

"From His mouth comes a sharp sword with which to strike down the nations, and He will rule them with a rod of iron. He will tread the winepress of the fury of the wrath of God the Almighty. On His robe and on His thigh, He has a name written, King of kings and Lord of lords."[21]

He's also coming back to save and to restore:

"So, Christ, having been offered once to bear the sins of many, will appear a second time, not to deal with sin but to save those who are eagerly waiting for Him."[22]

"Thus, says the Lord, the God of Israel: Write in a book all the words that I have spoken to you. For behold, days are coming, declares the Lord, when I will restore the fortunes of My people, Israel and Judah, says the Lord, and I will bring them back to the land that I gave to their fathers, and they shall take possession of it."[23]

"Thus, says the Lord: Behold, I will restore the fortunes of the tents of Jacob and have compassion on his dwellings; the city shall be rebuilt on its mound, and the palace shall stand where it used to be."[24]

"For to us a Child is born, to us, a Son is given; and the government shall be upon His shoulder, and His name shall be called Wonderful Counselor, Mighty God, Everlasting Father, Prince of Peace. Of the increase of His government and of peace, there will be no end, on the throne of David and over His kingdom, to establish it and to uphold it with justice and with righteousness from this time forth and forevermore. The zeal of the Lord of hosts will do this."[25]

In this Kingdom that Jesus establishes on the earth, the nations who formerly came against this City of the Great King will then flow to it like a sanctified Hajj for the Feast of Tabernacles.

---

21 Revelation 19:15-16
22 Hebrews 9:28
23 Jeremiah 30:2-3
24 Jeremiah 30:18
25 Isaiah 9:6-7

"Then everyone who survives of all the nations that have come against Jerusalem shall go up year after year to worship the King, the Lord of hosts, and to keep the Feast of Booths. And if any of the families of the earth do not go up to Jerusalem to worship the King, the Lord of hosts, there will be no rain on them. And if the family of Egypt does not go up and present themselves, then on them there shall be no rain; there shall be the plague with which the Lord afflicts the nations that do not go up to keep the Feast of Booths."[26]

"It shall come to pass in the latter days that the mountain of the house of the Lord shall be established as the highest of the mountains, and it shall be lifted up above the hills; and peoples shall flow to it, and many nations shall come, and say: 'Come, let us go up to the mountain of the Lord, to the house of the God of Jacob, that He may teach us His ways and that we may walk in His paths.' For out of Zion shall go forth the law, and the word of the Lord from Jerusalem."[27]

Why is it necessary to understand that Jesus will be coming back to Jerusalem? Because it's right that we have a confident expectation of what is going to happen when He returns. Jesus told us beforehand. But it's especially crucial with the existence of anti-Semitism because we don't want to make disciples who are ignorant about these things—lest in their ignorance, they spread an expectation about God that contributes toward the negative view some people hold toward the Jewish people. Our Jewish Jesus is going to rule from Jerusalem, just like the Jewish prophets said He would.

While this can seem like a lot of information at first, as we familiarize ourselves more and more, it becomes simpler and more straightforward. Elementary school is difficult when we are children, but as we go on to complete middle school and high school, elementary academics become easy for us. In the same way, as servants with a message, we need to familiarize ourselves with that message. We need

---

[26] Zechariah 14:16-18
[27] Micah 4:1-2

to understand it well enough that we would be able to teach it simply, to a child.

KINDNESS AND SEVERITY

The good news is very divisive. It can become tempting to leave out challenging aspects of God's character to secure a more positive response from people, but this often does more harm than good. Many Christians have reinterpreted plain Scriptures to accommodate the sins of a particular group they are trying to reach. By doing this, some believers have lost their own stability in the faith. We must embrace both easy things and challenging things the Bible has to say. We must herald God's kindness as well as His severity.[28]

> "There are some things in them that are hard to understand, which the ignorant and unstable twist to their own destruction, as they do the other Scriptures. You, therefore, beloved, knowing this beforehand, take care that you are not carried away with the error of lawless people and lose your own stability."[29]

Our appeal is not dishonest or underhanded. We don't intentionally keep back things that are hard to hear. We want to help set people up to have the right expectations about who God is and what He does. We don't want to tamper with God's Word. We need to make clear statements of truth with a clear conscience before the Lord. Let's stay far away from reinterpreting plain sayings of God for the sake of "influence." One great way to avoid losing our stability regarding sound doctrine is by subjecting ourselves to God's Word within a community that can ask, "Where in the Bible does it say that?"

> "Our appeal does not spring from error or impurity or any attempt to deceive."[30]

> "But we have renounced disgraceful, underhanded ways. We refuse to practice cunning or to tamper with God's word, but by open statement of the truth we would

---

28   Romans 11:22
29   2 Peter 3:16-17
30   1 Thessalonians 2:3

commend ourselves to everyone's conscience in the sight of God."[1]

THE SIMPLICITY OF RELATIONSHIP

Our role as servants commissioned by the King is to not only deliver a message, but to urge implore the lost to come and "taste and see that the Lord is good."[2] Doing so requires time, genuine relationship, patience, and the Holy Spirit. This way, we are facilitating opportunities for God to demonstrate Himself to them over time, rather than relying on our own ability to preach the Gospel unto their conversion.

> "And I, when I came to you, brothers, did not come proclaiming to you the testimony of God with lofty speech or wisdom. For I decided to know nothing among you except Jesus Christ and Him crucified. And I was with you in weakness and in fear and much trembling, and my speech and my message were not in plausible words of wisdom, but in demonstration of the Spirit and of power, so that your faith might not rest in the wisdom of men but in the power of God."[3]

This is something that requires humility and accepting our limitations within our responsibility before God. The goal of our preaching is for people to see the glory of God in the face of Jesus and give Him the praise that's due His name. It's not for us to praise our own effectiveness in ministry. There is a distinct difference.

> "For what we proclaim is not ourselves, but Jesus Christ as Lord, with ourselves as your servants for Jesus' sake. For God, who said, "Let light shine out of darkness," has shone in our hearts to give the light of the knowledge of the glory of God in the face of Jesus Christ."[4]

What we proclaim is not ourselves. This liberating truth relieves the pressure from us to have to perform effectively or preach convincingly enough for the lost to come to Christ. It secures the place of humility

---

[1] 2 Corinthians 4:2
[2] Psalm 34:8
[3] 1 Corinthians 2:1-5
[4] 2 Corinthians 4:5-6

where God remains God, and man remains man, and each is doing their part according to their abilities.

> "If we forget that it is God's prerogative to give results when the Gospel is preached, we shall start to think that it is our responsibility to secure them. And if we forget that only God can give faith, we shall start to think that the making of converts depends...not on God, but on us, and that the decisive factor is the way in which we evangelize."[5]

> "But we have this treasure in jars of clay, to show that the surpassing power belongs to God and not to us."[6]

There are significant differences between merely delivering a sermon and actively discipling a lost person toward Jesus over time and in a relationship. It's the difference between having a letter and being the letter.

> "You are a letter from Christ delivered by us, written not with ink but with the Spirit of the living God, not on tablets of stone but on tablets of human hearts."[7]

If we set out merely to preach a sermon, that's all we'll end up doing. But if we go out to bring in brothers and sisters to worship God in the age to come, then that's what we'll accomplish. The former employs one technique based on an underlying value that, whether it's accepted or rejected, the job is finished when the Gospel is presented. The latter use anything necessary, in the relational context of a partnership with God's Spirit, to compel the person to the Lord.

Discipleship undertaken this way will often be very uncomfortable and inconvenient. But nervous obedience in partnership with God is far more effective than simply telling the good news to people we choose arbitrarily. And it will require much more of us than just dispensing good theology. Our role is not merely to make people accountable for the information. They already are accountable[8] and will be damned.[9]

---

5   Packer, J.I. (2012 reprint). *Evangelism and the sovereignty of God*. Westmont, IL: Inter-Varsity Press.

6   2 Corinthians 4:7

7   2 Corinthians 3:3

8   Romans 1:18-19

9   John 3:18,36

Our role is to do everything we can to implore people on behalf of Christ to be reconciled to God. It may get emotional. And that's good.

> "Therefore, if anyone is in Christ, he is a new creation. The old has passed away; behold, the new has come. All this is from God, who through Christ reconciled us to Himself and gave us the ministry of reconciliation; that is, in Christ God was reconciling the world to Himself, not counting their trespasses against them, and entrusting to us the message of reconciliation. Therefore, we are ambassadors for Christ, God making His appeal through us. We implore you on behalf of Christ, be reconciled to God. For our sake, He made Him to be sin who knew no sin so that in Him, we might become the righteousness of God."[10]

We are ambassadors of the coming Kingdom. No one, Abraham included, has seen it yet.[11] But we know the King. We are His representatives. We are diplomatic officials of the highest rank, sent on behalf of the sovereign ruler of a Kingdom to negotiate terms of peace. The definition of an ambassador is a beautiful and biblical description of every blood-bought Christian.

Part of our responsibility as Christians is to cultivate the kind of relationship with the Lord where Jesus needs only to ask us to do something, and we joyfully do it. We need to trust Him so much that we will do anything He asks of us, even if it's difficult, awkward, socially unacceptable, or dangerous. Waiting on God and working alongside Him is the most compelling thing we can do. Apart from the dynamic, relational camaraderie with Jesus, all we have is confidence in the flesh and security in methods, tactics, and approaches.

DEMONSTRATION

> "And my speech and my message were not in plausible words of wisdom, but in demonstration of the Spirit and of power, so that your faith might not rest in the wisdom of men but in the power of God."[12]

---

10   2 Corinthians 5:17-21
11   Hebrews 11:39-40
12   1 Corinthians 2:4-5

In my experience, I have found that what Paul wrote about a demonstration of the Spirit and power is the most effective means by which men become convinced to listen to the Gospel. Sharing a word of knowledge or a prophetic word[13] can be incredibly practical to reach the heart of a calloused person. Paul testifies to the power of the Holy Spirit for evangelism: "But if all prophesy, and an unbeliever or outsider enters, he is convicted by all, he is called to account by all, the secrets of his heart are disclosed, and so, falling on his face, he will worship God and declare that God really is among you."[14]

How amazing would that be to bring a prophetic word during evangelism and the person you're sharing with is cut to the heart and declares that God really is with you! As servants who have been sent by the Master, it's in our best interest to employ everything we have access to through God in our attempts to bring people to the Lord. It would be silly for us to call someone to salvation with confidence only in our approach, method, or content. Unless the Spirit of God breathes on our attempt, our cute sermon will have no real power to bring someone to conviction or repentance.

When I lived in New Zealand as a young man, a group of us would go out on Friday nights after our evening prayer meetings and share the Gospel with strangers on the street. One night, I met a very drunk teenager who was talking with my friend, Dan. I stood nearby, praying for him while Dan shared. While I was praying, I could not shake the image of a cactus from my mind. I just kept picturing the little potted plant. I figured, "What the heck, maybe it has some meaning to this kid." So, I shared with him, and he instantly became amazed at what I said. He asked me, "How the (expletive) did you know that?" I said, "Know what?" "About my hobby," he said, "How did you know that I love cactuses?" I didn't know this guy loved cacti. The image just popped up in my head, so I told him. But for this kid, he understood at that moment that God cared about him and even knew his hobbies. In his mind, this affirmed everything we had been telling him about God. I learned that being sensitive to the Holy Spirit can be very useful in evangelism.

---

13   1 Corinthians 12:8,10
14   1 Corinthians 14:24-25

Another gift that serves well in evangelism is the gift of healing.[15] The disciples were doing many miracles, and believers were added to the Lord.[16] In one case, Jesus confirms His message to a disbelieving religious crowd by performing a healing miracle:

> "And He was preaching the word to them. And they came, bringing to Him a paralytic carried by four men... and when Jesus saw their faith, He said to the paralytic, 'Son, your sins are forgiven.' Now some of the scribes were sitting there, questioning in their hearts, 'Why does this man speak like that? He is blaspheming! Who can forgive sins but God alone? And immediately Jesus, perceiving in His spirit that they thus questioned within themselves, said to them, 'Why do you question these things in your hearts? Which is easier, to say to the paralytic, 'Your sins are forgiven,' or to say, 'Rise, take up your bed and walk'? But that you may know that the Son of Man has authority on earth to forgive sins'—He said to the paralytic, 'I say to you, rise, pick up your bed, and go home.' And he rose and immediately picked up his bed and went out before them all so that they were all amazed and glorified God, saying, 'We never saw anything like this!'"[17]

Religious men who already made up their minds about Jesus' deity were amazed by His authority and glorified God when He healed a paralyzed man. Perhaps in our day too, the people who are convinced that healing has ceased may have a similar response when they actually see it happen. We should leave room for this kind of demonstration of the Holy Spirit. Some people question if the gifts are still operational nowadays. I wonder—how we could effectively minister to the lost if they weren't? If we disregard what Scripture says about the spiritual gifts, we will have to rely more heavily on our own abilities. In that case, what will our confidence be in? The surpassing greatness of power belongs to God and not to us.

"Now you are the body of Christ and individually members

---

15   1 Corinthians 12:9
16   Acts 5:12-16; 19:11
17   Mark 2:2-3,5-12

> of it. And God has appointed in the church first apostles, second prophets, third teachers, then miracles, then gifts of healing, helping, administrating, and various kinds of tongues. Are all apostles? Are all prophets? Are all teachers? Do all work miracles? Do all possess gifts of healing? Do all speak with tongues? Do all interpret? But earnestly desire the higher gifts."[18]

I don't want us to paint a picture of Christians as masters of spiritual gifts, wielding power like we're the ones in control. It's God who empowers us as He sees fit. Not everyone is given a specific spiritual gift.

> "Now there are varieties of gifts, but the same Spirit; and there are varieties of service, but the same Lord; and there are varieties of activities, but it is the same God who empowers them all in everyone. To each is given the manifestation of the Spirit for the common good."[19]

Paul clearly says that not all work miracles or have the gift of healing or speaking in tongues. So, confining our understanding of the demonstration of God's power to only include spiritual gifts can be really limiting to our efforts. We need to consider the other ways God chooses to demonstrate His ability in partnership with our obedience. God loves to show His power in many ways, whether or not He chooses to utilize a believer's spiritual gifts.

The Lord loves to reveal Himself to people through our relationships with the lost. I have witnessed and heard many incredible accounts of lost people being transformed by God as they are simply led by a believer to read, obey, and share the Bible.

It's an incredibly useful and straightforward way for unbelievers to build a history of experiencing Jesus even before they believe. A friend of mine in Iran told me a story of a man who decided to stop abusing his wife after reading in Genesis 2 that God made both man and woman in His image. No spiritual gifts were employed, but that man experienced a demonstration of God's power to transform his life simply by reading a passage in Genesis and committing to obey it.

---

18 1 Corinthians 12:27-31a
19 1 Corinthians 12:4-7

I have personally seen God do this while living in Iraqi Kurdistan. One morning, my wife and I were praying with tears for someone to disciple. We had lived there for only nine months and hadn't made enough progress with the language to have very many meaningful relationships with locals, but there were a few English-speaking people we could engage with.

Later, that very same day, out of nowhere, my Kurdish teacher called me and asked if he could come over just to hang out. Before this, we had kept our interaction primarily centered around language learning. He came over that afternoon for some tea. While we were talking the prayer call echoed from behind my house. At that time, my official address was, "Behind Azadi Mosque." We were right under the minaret, which is what has the loud speaker mounted to it. So, it was annoyingly loud, and my teacher got up to pray.

When he sat back down at the table after praying, I asked him if he believed God heard his prayers. He told me, "Of course!" But when I asked him if God answered his prayers, he said, "How can God answer prayers?" He said it as more of a statement than a question. I asked him if he wanted to hear God speak to him, and he said, "Of course!"

So, he agreed to read Genesis 1 with me and answer a few questions I had for him afterward. We did the same thing the following week with Genesis chapter two. It was during second week when I witnessed something miraculous happen, something I would consider to be God demonstrating His power. The questions I asked my friend were:

> 1) What did you learn about God from this passage?
>
> 2) What did you learn about mankind from this passage?
>
> 3) How will you obey God from this passage?
>
> 4) Who will you share this story with?

His answer to the second question thrilled me! He said that he learned that men and women were created as equals. This is a miracle all by itself. Most conservative Muslims would not readily admit that women are equal to men. Then I asked him how he will obey God from the passage, and what he told me excited me even more. It was hard to contain my happiness. He told me that if his sister was his equal, he was going to help her with house chores from that time forward. You have to understand, there is not a single Kurdish man I know who cleans his own room or makes his own bed. To them, that's women's work. But my teacher said, "From now on, I will clean my own room and make my own bed!" Imagine the witness of the Word to his sister, through his own eager obedience!

I had given my teacher my presentation of the Gospel on one or two occasions before that day, and nothing changed. But when he read and obeyed the Bible himself, God transformed his mind and changed a centuries-old belief that men were superior to women in a just couple of minutes. This is why it's so important to labor with God in making disciples, relying on Him alone, "that our faith might not rest in the wisdom of man, but in the power of God!"[20]

If the ultimate goal is for God to demonstrate Himself to the lost, what part do we actually play? We pray for them,[21] appeal to them, and implore them.[22] We invite people[23] and compel them to come in.[24] We proclaim Him who called us.[25] We reason with them, explain to them, let God prove Himself to them, persuade them.[26] We destroy arguments raised against the knowledge of God.[27] And we warn them.[28] This is no passive endeavor. It requires action and empathy for the lost that can only be wrought by connecting with the Lord, who has compassion on them.

"When He saw the crowds, He had compassion for them, because they were harassed and helpless, like sheep without a shepherd. Then He said to His disciples, 'The harvest is plentiful, but the laborers are few; therefore, pray earnestly to the Lord of the harvest to send out laborers into His harvest.'"[29]

---

20 1 Corinthians 2:5
21 Matthew 9:36-38
22 2 Corinthians 5:20
23 Matthew 22:4
24 Luke 14:23
25 Matthew 10:27; 1 Peter 2:9
26 Acts 17:2-4
27 2 Corinthians 10:5
28 Colossians 1:28
29 Matthew 9:36-38

The Lord's response to lost and shepherdess people is compassion and action. God's compassion results in His asking us to pray. So, we pray. And He answers our prayer by sending those of us who have been praying as laborers. It's an incredible dance between God's sovereignty and man's responsibility.

Application

A good question to ask when at this point is: How do we employ this knowledge when it really matters? How does this play out in real-time with our colleagues at work or classmates at school? Is there any practical application for this theology when I'm interacting with my unbelieving friends and acquaintances?

Jesus laid out a straightforward plan of action for making disciples in a new place. It's one of the most precise pictures we see of the practical strategy that God gave for His disciples to follow. So, we'll look at this passage and draw out a few key points that address these questions.

> "After this, the Lord appointed seventy-two others and sent them on ahead of Him, two by two, into every town and place where He Himself was about to go. And He said to them, 'The harvest is plentiful, but the laborers are few. Therefore, pray earnestly to the Lord of the harvest to send out laborers into His harvest. Go your way; behold, I am sending you out as lambs in the midst of wolves. Carry no moneybag, no knapsack, no sandals, and greet no one on the road. Whatever house you enter, first say, 'Peace be to this house!' And if a son of peace is there, your peace will rest upon him. But if not, it will return to you. And remain in the same house, eating and drinking what they provide, for the laborer deserves his wages. Do not go from house to house. Whenever you enter a town, and they receive you, eat what is set before you. Heal the sick in it and say to them, 'The kingdom of God has come near to you.' But whenever you enter a town and they do not receive you, go into its streets and say, 'Even the dust of your town that clings to our feet we wipe off against you. Nevertheless, know this, that the kingdom of God has come near.'"[1]

---

1   Luke 10:1-11

With Someone

In this passage, we are instructed to go out in pairs. In my experience, it is far more encouraging to have another person to minister with. It also serves as an accountability and safety measure. There is a definite advantage in going two-by-two. Of course, it can't always be done. But when it's in our power, we will do well to minister alongside someone else.

The first directive Jesus gives to the pairs of disciples is to pray. We are to pray for laborers to be sent into the harvest field. Pray for the people of peace Jesus described. People who, when they come to Christ, will make disciples in their own communities. They are (for now) unsaved men and women who open the door for us into their community. These are people who need no convincing, they already want to hear the good news we came to bring because the Holy Spirit has been preparing them. Let's pray the Lord leads us to them.

As Sheep

Next, we're told that we are being sent out as sheep among wolves. In other words, we're being led into danger. Imagine going into the less-than-reputable part of town. Or to a place where the majority of people are from a different ethnicity than you. How uncomfortable and inadequate would you feel in that context? That's the point! Think about it. When we are nervous and feel unsafe, we pray. When we are sent into places that are dangerous and scary, we depend on God. And when we're open to hearing and obeying Him, it's easy for Him to use us to find and make disciples. It may be an excellent idea for a church's homegrown to "step over the tracks," if you will, into an unfamiliar area and see what God will do with your willingness and obedience.

We are then instructed not to bring anything with us. No bag of clothes. No money. And we are told not to stop to greet those along the way. We leave everything behind, and we don't get distracted. In our day, we may want to add leaving the phone in the car to that list. Continuing with the example of a home group going into the more dangerous part of town, consider what it would be like to do that without your phone and without money for lunch. When we're hungry and tired and have no money, we cannot just go to a restaurant. And we can't use UberEats. We will have to find a person who is willing to invite us to rest and eat with them (which is admittedly much more comfortable in the Middle East than in America—but give it a try anyway).

When we do find someone willing to extend their hospitality to us, we are told to enter their house and stay with that person or family. We don't need to go from house-to-house. The Lord has led us to this person of peace, this gatekeeper into the community. We should honor him or her by staying with them and eating whatever they provide. And we don't have to be shy about accepting a home-cooked meal. It could be more offensive to them if we refuse it. Plus, the Lord said that the laborers deserve their wages. We are to bless their homes and be a blessing to them in their homes. And if their response is favorable, we bless them more and begin to share the Gospel with them.

Serving the needs of the community is one of the best ways to build a reputation as a reliable and trustworthy person. This way, people are not wary and skeptical of us but are welcoming and hospitable. It's easier to make disciples in a town that wants you there. It may not be sustainable for your home group to walk around a new city each week following the same approach. So consider the needs of a particular community. Ask the person who showed you favor and hospitality what the needs there are. Find out who is responsible there and ask what ways you can meet those needs. You'll be surprised by the opportunities for long-term engagement and disciple-making that open up through simple service.

The final instruction Jesus gives His followers is to wipe the dust off our feet from the towns that do not welcome us. It may be hard to walk away from a place you set your heart on, but that is Jesus' prerogative. It's ultimately His responsibility. He is the Lord of the harvest, and if He has not yet prepared a people for our coming, we should move on and find a place He has prepared for us. I don't see any reason why the simplicity of Jesus' instructions to the first-century disciples would be any less useful for us today. It doesn't need to be complicated.

Unless God

Unless the Father draws a person to His Son, they will not be saved.

Unless the Lord builds His house, our labors are in vain. By understanding this, we will alleviate unnecessary pressure we feel when witnessing. The pressure to convert someone is not our shoulders. It's on God's.

The verse below sets the tone for understanding the process of man's salvation. We love because He first loved us.[2] God initiates the whole thing with love while we were His enemies.[3] It's like the parable of the wedding feast: Everything is prepared, all you have to do is show up!

"And we know that for those who love God all things work together for good, for those who are called according to His purpose. For those whom He foreknew, He also predestined to be conformed to the image of His Son, in order that He might be the firstborn among many brothers. And those whom He predestined He also called, and those whom He called He also justified, and those whom He justified He also glorified."[4]

You were known before you were made and were predestined for adoption. The Father drew you to Jesus, and God's kindness brought you to repentance. He made you into a new creation. You believed and were baptized.

In his book *Evangelism and the Sovereignty of God*, J.I. Packer succinctly states, "You do not pat yourself on the back for having been at length mastered by the insistent Christ...You have never told God that, while you were grateful for the means and the opportunities of grace that He gave you, you realize that you have to thank, not Him, but yourself for the fact that you responded to His call."[5]

If you cannot bear God's wrath for a person, you cannot save them. If you cannot make them a new creature or cause them to be born again from God's Spirit, then you cannot save them. And isn't that a relief? You cannot save a human soul. You are not responsible for converting anyone you share the Gospel with. Of course, we want people to come to the saving knowledge of God, but our only role is to invite and compel them according to what He has done to prove

---

[2] 1 John 4:19

[3] Romans 5:8,10

[4] Romans 8:28-30

[5] Packer, J.I. (2012 reprint). *Evangelism and the sovereignty of God*. Westmont, IL: InterVarsity Press.

His great love to us. But we leave the burden of converting a soul to God. We are expected to proclaim the Gospel faithfully, whether people respond well or not. Even if no one ever answers.

As Christians, it's not our job to convict, convert, or condemn the lost—that's God's job. Our job is to demonstrate our crucified Messiah. We invite men and women into reconciliation with God.

Again, unless the Lord draws someone to Himself, nothing happens. And this is why we must be careful not to package an effective method to market as a one-size-fits-all approach. Often in our excitement of finding something that works well for us, we want it to work well for others too, which is excellent. We just need to be careful not to over-emphasize it, as if it is the only way that works.

A SERVANT WORTHY OF THE CALLING

Toward the end of each chapter, we will borrow some of the fatherly advice Paul gives to Timothy, his young apprentice in the faith. For now, we'll start with Paul's description of a worker (or servant) who has been approved.

In the second chapter of Paul's second letter to Timothy, he writes: "Do your best to present yourself to God as one approved, a worker who has no need to be ashamed, rightly handling the word of truth."[6] Already this sentence is packed with useful direction for Timothy and for us as well. But Paul gives even more clarity in his letter to the church in Ephesus:

"I, therefore, a prisoner for the Lord, urge you to walk in a manner worthy of the calling to which you have been called, with all humility and gentleness, with patience, bearing with one another in love, eager to maintain the unity of the Spirit in the bond of peace."[7]

We are to present ourselves to God as one approved, to walk in a manner worthy of the calling. Paul then goes on to name the qualities he has in mind, which is helpful to know what we're aiming for when we are looking to qualifications for ministry. Paul names humility, gentleness, patience, bearing with one another, and eagerly maintaining unity as the premier attributes of one who is worthy of his or her calling.

---

6   2 Timothy 2:15
7   Ephesians 4:1-3

> "And so, from the day we heard, we have not ceased to pray for you, asking that you may be filled with the knowledge of His will in all spiritual wisdom and understanding so as to walk in a manner worthy of the Lord, fully pleasing to Him: bearing fruit in every good work and increasing in the knowledge of God."[8]

It's significant that in this passage, Paul includes "bearing fruit" in his description of one who is walking in a manner worthy of the Lord. One of the marks of maturity among Jesus' disciples is our ability to bear fruit in making more disciples.

Because of the spiritual nature of discipleship, it's not quite as easy to gauge whether or not we are working hard in it. Nevertheless, Paul urges his young companion that "It is the hard-working farmer who ought to have the first share of the crops."[9] We need to bring the mindset of a hard worker into our disciple-making strategies, and we can look to the work ethic of a farmer for inspiration.

> "Train yourself for godliness; for while bodily training is of some value, godliness is of value in every way, as it holds promise for the present life and also for the life to come."[10]

I love this passage. In the same way we train our bodies with programs like CrossFit or Zumba, we can prepare ourselves for obedience to Jesus. It's intentional, disciplined, and yields results. We don't always hear appeals from the pulpit to train ourselves in godliness, but to Paul, this was very important to impart to a young disciple.

> "Command and teach these things. Let no one despise you for your youth, but set the believers an example in speech, in conduct, in love, in faith, in purity. Until I come, devote yourself to the public reading of Scripture, to exhortation, to teaching. Do not neglect the gift you have, which was given you by prophecy when the council of elders laid their hands on you. Practice these things, immerse yourself in them, so that all may see your progress. Keep a close watch

---

8 Colossians 1:9-10
9 2 Timothy 2:6
10 1 Timothy 4:7-8

on yourself and on the teaching. Persist in this, for by so doing, you will save both yourself and your hearers."[11]

Notice the practical and actionable instructions Paul is giving. Train yourself. Be an example. Devote yourself to the Scripture. Do not neglect your gifts. Practice. Keep a close watch. Persist.

> "As for you, always be sober-minded, endure suffering, do the work of an evangelist, fulfill your ministry."[12]

It's the pastoral kindness of Paul to prepare Timothy with the expectation that doing the work of evangelism will be accompanied by a great deal of suffering—much as his own evangelistic efforts had been. While this might include suffering persecution, I think what Paul has in mind here is to suffer through the hard work of disciple-making.

Making many disciples doesn't just "happen" simply because we're Christians. Discipleship doesn't rub off on your neighbor through social osmosis. It requires hard work, endurance, patience, persistence, practice, humility, bearing each other's burdens, eagerly maintaining unity. It's challenging and costly; that's why Paul is urging Timothy to "share in the suffering, as a good soldier."[13] If we are to be faithful servants and stewards of the mysteries of God, we will do well to take the fatherly advice of Paul to heart.

FRUITLESSNESS

During the first eight years following my salvation, I can recount sharing the Gospel with a little over 630 people. In America, Australia, New Zealand, Philippines, Fiji, Brazil, Scotland, Ireland, Turkey, Israel, and most recently, Iraqi Kurdistan.

There were lawyers and judges, businessmen, religious leaders, members of cults, witches, hair stylists, family members, friends, police officers, prisoners—people from all walks of life. It happened everywhere: bus stops, movie theaters, rock climbing gyms, restaurants, boardwalks, huts, homes, hot pools, karaoke pubs, parking lots, grocery stores, tattoo shops, skate parks, and even one time while standing on a chair in the mall. I spent hours carefully crafting my

---

11 1 Timothy 4:11-16
12 2 Timothy 4:5
13 2 Timothy 2:3

articulation of the Gospel so that if I only had a couple minutes, I could be as clear and precise as the times when I had hours.

I tried every sort of approach. I used my testimony, a flip chart, and made my own Gospel tracts. I drew with chalk on the sidewalk and even bought a soccer cone that I turned into a megaphone but never actually used.

Some of these interactions were incredibly positive. Others were discouragingly negative. I am aware of only two people who gave their lives to the Lord as a result of my witnessing. Only two out of six hundred and thirty! And neither of them was interested in following up with me to read the Bible.

I believe that God may at times ordain seasons of apparent fruitlessness for our own good so that we come to accept that the decisive factor in man's salvation is not the surpassing greatness of our methods or approach, but God Himself. This has helped to solidify in me the reality that unless the Lord builds His house, we labor in vain. By God withholding apparent fruitfulness for a season, it secures our long-term dependency on Him and His active involvement in the process of each person coming to faith in His Son.

More than anything, it checks my motivation for making disciples. I've noticed that the times I feel most anxious with my apparent fruitlessness is when I am preoccupied with thoughts of validating myself to others. But when my motivation to bear fruit is purely to please Jesus, I'm not anxious at all when I'm not seeing the results I daydream of. Considering experiences like my own, we shouldn't be afraid to scrutinize our approach and examine our fruitfulness to determine whether we are effectively obeying the Great Commission. Our methods of evangelism may need to be tested and challenged—especially if all that's left in their wake is an underwhelming number of lost people being discipled.

This is a good reminder. While we must be seeking to bear measurable fruit and reproduce the Gospel, we also need to bear in mind that we plant, and we water, but it's ultimately God who gives the growth. "So, neither he who plants nor he who waters is anything, but only God who gives the growth."[14]

---

14   1 Corinthians 3:7

Closing

There's a reason why I put so much emphasis on announcing the Gospel. Because we can do all the humanitarian work we want, build all the hospitals and schools we want, but if we aren't making disciples, those healthy, well-educated people will go straight to Hell when they die. It should be no comfort to us at all that we can relieve suffering only in this age while letting human beings slip through our fingers into torment and agony in the age to come.

Every Christian is a servant of Christ and a steward of the mysteries of God. We have already been approved by God to be entrusted with the good news, and we have a responsibility to be faithful with it. We are ambassadors. We are letters written by God delivered to the lost. We are servants sent by the Master to compel to come in as many as we find so His house will be filled with guests. Whether we employ teaching, or miracles, or hospitality, or service, let's be people who will utilize anything and everything in our power to obey Jesus and help disciple the lost toward Him.

An Original Poem

Worthy is the Lamb because He was slain;
In the stead of humanity, and He took the blame.
Christ took the blow, Jesus Christ took the pain;
And it pleased the Father to crush the Son, for the glory of His name.
Now He is who is worthy, in His goodness we can trust;
Because we know the host of Heaven sings that God is always just.
He is just to judge since He was judged for us;
Our condemnation was in the cup that was swallowed by Jesus.
So it is right that we should praise Him, it is fitting we respond;
With worship for the Lamb whose praise goes on and on.

JORDAN SCOTT

SECTION II

THE URGENCY OF MAKING DISCIPLES

"Then the master of the house became angry and said to his servant, 'Go out quickly to the streets and lanes of the city, and bring in the poor and crippled and blind and lame.'"[1]

"Invite to the wedding feast as many as you find."[2]

This passage reveals to us the Lord's urgency for lost souls. "Go quickly! Invite as many as you find." He wants His house filled with those whom He has given the right to become children of God. And He wants us to go out and bring them in.

> "And the servant said, 'Sir, what you commanded has been done, and still there is room.' And the master said to the servant, 'Go out to the highways and hedges and compel people to come in, that my house may be filled.'"[3]

As we've seen in the previous chapter, we have a responsibility, not

---

1   Luke 14:21
2   Matthew 22:9
3   Luke 14:22-23

only to invite people but to compel them to come in. In a sermon on this parable, Charles Spurgeon once said, "Brother, I was not told merely to tell you and then go about my business. No; I am told to compel you to come in."[4] "Compel" is not a quiet little word. It's intense. It's intentional. The Bible is full of powerfully emotional phrases like this one. My favorite is in Paul's second letter to the Corinthians:

> "All this is from God, who through Christ reconciled us to Himself and gave us the ministry of reconciliation; that is, in Christ God was reconciling the world to Himself, not counting their trespasses against them, and entrusting to us the message of reconciliation. Therefore, we are ambassadors for Christ, God making His appeal through us. We implore you on behalf of Christ, be reconciled to God. For our sake He made Him to be sin who knew no sin so that in Him we might become the righteousness of God."[5]

Hear the deep emotion: "We *implore* you… *be reconciled* to God! He's pleading with them. *Begging* them. *"Please, whatever you do, be reconciled to God!"* I picture a man on his knees, hugging the legs of a lost person, pleading like a dying man for Him to come to the saving knowledge of Jesus.

Why? Why beg someone to come to Christ? What's the urgency?

What happens to a person who doesn't hear the Gospel and come to Christ may be the most compelling reason we have to declare it to them with great urgency. "Whoever believes in the Son has eternal life; whoever does not obey the Son shall not see life, but the wrath of God remains on him."[6] If the servants stay home, the lost don't come to the banquet. If we don't preach, they don't hear. If they don't understand the Gospel and fall in love with God's Son, the wrath of God remains on them.

SELFIES AND WRATH

If you saw a man walking backward toward the edge of the Grand

---

[4] Read the full sermon in Appendix A
[5] 2 Corinthians 5:18-21
[6] John 3:36

Canyon trying to snap a quick photo with his selfie-stick, would you say anything to him? Would anyone ever entertain the idea of staying quiet while a man walked blindly to his death? Of course not! Eternity in Hell is far more terrifying than plummeting off a cliff. Yet, how often do we speak up to warn others not to go to Hell?

This chapter will help remind us what it was like to be damned—what it's like to deserve the wrath of God so that we may receive greater concern for those on whom the wrath of God still remains. We'll start by looking at what Jesus says about Hell.

> "There was a rich man who was clothed in purple and fine linen and who feasted sumptuously every day. And at his gate was laid a poor man named Lazarus, covered with sores, who desired to be fed with what fell from the rich man's table. Moreover, even the dogs came and licked his sores. The poor man died and was carried by the angels to Abraham's side. The rich man also died and was buried, and in Hades, being in torment, he lifted up his eyes and saw Abraham far off and Lazarus at his side. And he called out, 'Father Abraham, have mercy on me, and send Lazarus to dip the end of his finger in water and cool my tongue, for I am in anguish in this flame.' But Abraham said, 'Child, remember that you in your lifetime received your good things, and Lazarus in like manner bad things; but now he is comforted here, and you are in anguish. And besides all this, between us and you, a great chasm has been fixed, in order that those who would pass from here to you may not be able, and none may cross from there to us.' And he said, 'Then I beg you, father, to send him to my father's house—for I have five brothers—so that he may warn them, lest they also come into this place of torment.' But Abraham said, 'They have Moses and the Prophets; let them hear them.' And he said, 'No, father Abraham, but if someone goes to them from the dead, they will repent.' He said to him, 'If they do not hear Moses and the prophets, neither will they be convinced if someone should rise from the dead.'"[7]

---

7   Luke 16:19-31

In this account, Jesus describes hell as "a place of torment" and "anguish," where men hope to escape but cannot. The rich man begs for his family to be warned not to come there, but Abraham tells him the prophets were warning enough. This is a hard thing. But this is what Jesus believes about Hell. We do not have the freedom to hold a different view than His. It's a mark of maturity among Jesus' disciples that we embrace what He taught, even when it's difficult and painful.[8] When you imagine your family members suffering torment forever, it can become tempting to dismiss the subject of Hell or even intentionally contradict what the Bible teaches about it. But we cannot allow sentimentality to alter the clear words of Jesus regarding eternal punishment.

I live in a predominantly Muslim nation. Every time I drive through town, I pass a little shop where a man sits outside carving gravestones for his community. It grieves me to see this because, in a place where every person is taught from birth that God has no Son, every gravestone we see is marking the site of a person in anguish, begging for someone to warn their family not to come to that place of torment. And while it's painful to consider what awaits them for eternity, it's healthy for us to remember what's going to happen to our friends and neighbors if they don't hear the Gospel and repent. It can drive us into bearing more responsibility for warning our unreached neighbors to hide in Jesus before it's too late.

How many people do you know who do not love the Son of God? Each one of those people is on their way to an eternity of anguish and torment. And they deserve it. God does not owe them salvation. But take heart! If anyone is in Hell, it's because God is good and He judged correctly. No one is in Hell who doesn't deserve to be there. There will never be a person in Hell who doesn't deserve to be there. You can bank on that. God does not delight in the death of anyone created in His image.[9] He has proven that by crucifying His Son in the place of all who accept His free gift.

What really astonishes me is that we all deserve to be in Hell. All have sinned and fall short of the glory of God.[10] We sinned against

---

8 John 6:60,67-68
9 Ezekiel 33:11
10 Romans 2:12; 3:23

an eternal God. We deserve eternal punishment. But rather than punishing us, God vented His eternal wrath by punishing His eternally innocent Son, the Word of God made flesh.[11] It's important to remember here that Jesus and the Father are One; the Godhead engineered these means.[12] For those who accept this finished work of free grace, God is just and the justifier of the one who has faith in Him.[13] But if anyone rejects Him, there is no longer a sacrifice for sin but a terrifying expectation of judgment.[14]

If we would speak up to warn a man in Arizona not to step backward off a cliff, how much more should we be comfortable with warning our neighbors "not to come to this place of torment!" Our responsibility to the unbelieving person extends beyond just an invitation to the Gospel—it includes a warning that if they don't accept, they will have to face a just God on Judgment Day without Jesus, without His holy blood as their Advocate and Defender. We want more for them than that.

What Was in The Cup?

In the garden of Gethsemane, we see Jesus in prayer, sweating blood in agony, greatly distressed because of the cup He was given to drink.[15] We don't often see Jesus is such a disconcerting state. So, we have to ask: Why was the Lord in great agony and distress? Why was Jesus sweating drops of blood? Why did God in the flesh require angelic ministers to strengthen Him? What was in that cup?

This cup in the hand of the Lord is described as filled with foaming wine for the wicked of the earth to drink down to the dregs.[16] It is a cup of wrath and bowl of staggering.[17] A cup of horror and desolation.[18] Containing the wine of God's wrath, poured full strength into the cup of His anger.[19] It's the cup of the wine of the fury of His wrath.[20]

---

11 John 1:1-14
12 John 17:21-22
13 Romans 3:26
14 Hebrews 10:26-27
15 Matthew 26:36-39; Mark 14:32-36; Luke 22:39-44
16 Psalm 75:8
17 Isaiah 51:17,22
18 Ezekiel 23:33
19 Revelation 14:10
20 Revelation 16:19

Jesus drank the cup the nations deserve. The cup we deserve. The cup our loved ones and co-workers deserve. But for anyone who does not put their faith in Jesus and in Him drinking the cup for them, of course, they will have to drink it themselves for eternity! Fearing the wrath of God is good. It may even be the convincing reason for some hesitant person to thrust themselves upon the Rock.[21]

Hell is man's default destination. Rightly deserving punishment is the default position and sentence of every human being. Before we do any bad or good, we are bad. Like a man stuck chest-deep in a pit of mud, if he does nothing, he is still stuck in the mud. If someone walked by to save him, and he refused, he would remain stuck in the mud. In the same way, when Jesus offers to save someone from Hell, and they refuse, the wrath of God remains on them. If men are not distressed by the weight of their guilt, what need do they have for a savior? From what exactly does he need to be saved? It's right and often necessary to convince someone of their evil before the Good News becomes attractive to that person.

What prevents a person from coming to Christ and being forgiven? In my experience, I have noticed that humans do not like having to admit that we need to be forgiven. Jesus says that men will not come into the light for fear that their works will be exposed.[22] They do not realize that the God whose light exposes their sins is the same God who covers the shame of their nakedness.[23] Mankind hates Jesus because He requires them to admit their guilt and repent.[24] Throughout history, human beings have hated admitting guilt so much that we have seized the servants of God, treated them shamefully, and killed them rather than listen to them and repent.[25]

We need to tell these people that, without Jesus' right standing with God, man will be separated forever from the Author of life.[26] They will experience eternal suffering and torment in Hell.[27] Make no mistake, when the Bible talks about fire and the destruction of towns

---

21 Psalm 18:2,31; 31:3; 62:2,6; 89:26; Isaiah 43:6-8
22 John 3:19-20
23 Ezekiel 16:8-10
24 John 15:22
25 Matthew 22:6; Hebrews 11:36-38
26 2 Thessalonians 1:9
27 Matthew 25:41,46; 2 Peter 2:4; Revelation 19:20

like Gomorrah, they are serving as an example of those who suffer the punishment of eternal flames.[28]

Human beings are not unaware of our guilt before God. "For the wrath of God is revealed from heaven against all ungodliness and unrighteousness of men, who by their unrighteousness suppress the truth…what can be known about God is plain to mankind, because God has shown it to them. His attributes have been clearly perceived, ever since the creation of the world, in the things that have been made."[29] God's law is written on our hearts, and our consciences bear witness to us. We are all without excuse.[30] This truth makes it clear that evangelism is not about making people accountable for the information. It is about addressing guilty people, who are without excuse, and earnestly appealing to them, compelling them to come to God. And we need to be very considerate when we're doing this.

Because of the severity of what we're talking about, we need to tread carefully. There are plenty of Christians who can talk about Hell like they're glancing over tomorrow's weather predictions. We should not discuss what Hell is like and who deserves to go there without even expressing emotion. This lack of empathy is very dangerous. Talking about the eternal punishment of people made in God's image is a very weighty subject. If we desire to engage this topic removed from God's emotions toward the people who are going to Hell, it would be better if we didn't discuss the subject at all. God is not calloused about those who will suffer His eternal wrath. We cannot afford to be either.

> "Have I any pleasure in the death of the wicked, declares the Lord GOD, and not rather that he should turn from his way and live?"[31]

> For I have no pleasure in the death of anyone, declares the Lord GOD; so turn and live."[32]

> "The Lord is not slow to fulfill His promise as some count

---

28 Jude 1:7
29 Romans 1:19-21
30 Romans 2:15
31 Ezekiel 18:23,32
32 Ezekiel 33:11

> slowness, but is patient toward you, not wishing that any should perish, but that all should reach repentance."[33]
>
> "Or do you presume on the riches of His kindness and forbearance and patience, not knowing that God's kindness is meant to lead you to repentance? But because of your hard and impenitent heart, you are storing up wrath for yourself on the day of wrath when God's righteous judgment will be revealed."[34]

While God has always been and will always be the perfectly just judge who will never let the guilt go unpunished, He does not enjoy the death of the wicked. He would much rather that they repent and live. As we've addressed, He so desires not to punish guilty men for their sins, that He crucified His only Son in their place. This way, He can uphold His justice by punishing wickedness and His mercy by forgiving guilty people who put their faith in His Son's sacrifice. He is just, and the justifier of the wicked who put their trust in the crucified Messiah.[35] This is fantastic news for sinners! Understanding this on a deeply emotional level can really help fuel our evangelistic efforts. Here's an example from Charles Spurgeon:

> "If sinners will be damned, at least let them leap to hell over our dead bodies; and if they will perish, let them perish with our arms about their knees, imploring them to stay. If hell must be filled, at least let it be filled in the teeth of our excursions, and let not one go there unwarned and un-prayed for."[36]

The reason we preach Christ to lost people is that, like our God, we do not wish that any should perish but that all come to repentance. We get to be the ones who not only tell people about the great tragedy that awaits the sinner, we also get to tell them about the Savior, the only way out! We should let the guilty sinner know that God says, even to them, "Come now, let us reason together, says the

---

33   2 Peter 3:9
34   Romans 2:4-5
35   Romans 3:26
36   The source of this quote is unknown.

Lord: though your sins are like scarlet, they shall be as white as snow; though they are red like crimson, they shall become like wool."[37]

THE INNOCENT WILL WARN

God spoke through the prophet Ezekiel to the watchmen of Israel, saying that if God were to give a warning for a wicked people and the watchman did not warn them, the people would die for their iniquity—but their blood would be required at the watchman's hand, because he did not warn them.[38]

Before leaving Ephesus, Paul shared an emotional goodbye with the church there. During their farewell, he declared that he was, "innocent of the blood of all, for I did not shrink from declaring to you the whole counsel of God."[39] Paul said that he, like a good watchman, was free from this bloodguilt—implying that if he had not declared the whole counsel of God, he would be guilty of their blood. And so would we, if we withhold warnings from the lost today. Because Hell is real, and because Jesus is beautiful, we must love people enough to speak up and love God too much to stay quiet.

As followers of Jesus, we know that Judgment Day is coming. If we don't warn our lost neighbors, they will die in their sin, and their blood will be on our hands. If we desire to be "innocent of the blood of all," we, like Paul, need to "not shrink back from declaring the whole counsel of God." We need to become comfortable with warning our neighbors that if they don't hide from the wrath of God in Jesus now, there will be nowhere for them to hide from the wrath of Jesus when He returns. And woe to us, if we do not!

> "For if I preach the Gospel, that gives me no ground for boasting. For necessity is laid upon me. Woe to me if I do not preach the Gospel!"[40]

Paul says, anguish, distress, and affliction upon us if we do not preach the Gospel. He's basically cursing himself with great consequences if he neglects to give a faithful witness. This is a very heavy admonition that deserves to be heeded. Think about this in your own context.

---

37 Isaiah 1:18
38 Ezekiel 3:17-19; 33:1-9
39 Acts 20:26-27
40 1 Corinthians 9:16

What if you recited these words over yourself today? "Woe to me if I do not share the Gospel with my neighbor, Kevin. Affliction and distress to my soul if I shrink back from declaring the good news to my colleague, Samantha." How would that change the way we approach our daily rhythms and routines? And if we do this willingly, we will be rewarded.

> "For if I do this of my own will, I have a reward, but if not of my own will, I am still entrusted with a stewardship."[41]

JONAH AND PHILLIP

The book of Jonah shows very clearly the urgent nature of our task and God's urgency toward the lost. Years ago, God told Jonah, a Jewish prophet, to go to Nineveh (modern-day Mosul) and call out against it because of the evil of the people.[42] That man defied God's directive and fled from Him that he might escape the from the presence of the Lord.[43]

God appointed for a great fish to come and swallow the man after he had been cast overboard by his crew.[44] Three days inside the belly of a great fish was enough to humble him into prayerful submission to God.[45] The fish vomited him onto dry land, and immediately, the Lord told him again, "Arise and go to Nineveh."[46]

I would have thought a few days rest would be in order after such an incredibly terrifying few days at sea. Well, the God of Abraham didn't think so. There was such a great urgency in the heart of God for the men of Nineveh to hear His judgment of them, that He directed Jonah to go to to them immediately. The Lord desired that they might respond with repentance so He may relent from the disaster He was going to do to them.[47] There were 120,000 people in Nineveh at the time[48] and all of them, right up to the king himself, repented for

---

41 1 Corinthians 9:17
42 Jonah 1:1-2
43 Jonah 1:3
44 Jonah 1:12,15,17
45 Jonah 2:1,10
46 Jonah 3:1-3
47 Jonah 3:10
48 Jonah 4:11

their sins and turned to the Lord.[49] They fasted, prayed, and humbled themselves before God.[50]

Jonah's disobedience ought to serve as an example to us. For me, it's like holding a mirror up to my face. I've never been a prophet or preached to an entire city, but I have refused God's clear directives. And I have felt the distress in my soul as a result. We all need to scrutinize ourselves to find if we, like Jonah, try to wiggle out of our responsibility to preach the good news to the lost.

In contrast to this story is another: when Philip baptized the man from Ethiopia. I believe it's a great example of urgency and obedience. It teaches the rightness of baptizing new Christians immediately when they believe, and it serves as a fascinating case study for cross-cultural evangelism.

When the Lord told Phillip to rise and go toward the road connecting Jerusalem to Gaza, Acts 8:27 says that Philip rose and went. No hesitation—a sharp contrast to the response we see from the prophet Jonah a few hundred years prior. When the Lord clarified further that Philip should join the man traveling on the road, he was so quick and intentional to obey, he literally ran to catch the moving chariot. This is something I can relate to.

One day, while driving around Tauranga, New Zealand, listening to worship in the car, I felt an urge to get in the left lane. When I did, I noticed a man walking on the sidewalk, and I knew right then that I would be sharing the Gospel with him. The only problem was I couldn't find a place to park. I drove about a block and a half past him and finally found a parking space. Then I got out and sprinted that full distance because he had turned a corner and I was afraid I wouldn't be able to find him again. When I finally caught up to him, I got his attention, but I was so out of breath that I couldn't say anything to him.

He smiled and waited for me to catch my breath. When I could speak clearly, I told him Jesus loved him so much that he had me chase him down to tell him. He appreciated that a lot and smiled nearly the whole time we talked. He didn't want to give his life to the Lord then, but he told me he'd weigh it up. Not a terrible response. So, when I

---

49 Jonah 3:5
50 Jonah 3:6-9

read about Philip running down to meet the chariot of the Ethiopian, I smirk a little because I know what that's like. Though, Philip was probably in better condition than I was because it seems like he gets to talking right away and doesn't need to catch his breath.

To get back to the text, we read that "Philip opened his mouth."[51] A pretty clear indication that we too need to open our mouths when sharing the Gospel. It must be reflected in our lives and actions, but it cannot be clearly communicated without words. The verse continues as Philip overhears the man reading Isaiah and "beginning with this Scripture, he told him the good news about Jesus."

Like Stephen, Phillip was not a full-time missionary or evangelist. He too was given responsibility to distribute food to widows.[52] He serves as another example of a regular believer being used by God to advance His Gospel in incredible ways through elementary acts of obedience.

The Highways and Hedges

It's interesting to watch the progression of the Master's commands each time He sends His servants out in the parable of the wedding feast. The first time, the Master sent His servants to inform those who were invited to the wedding feast. Those invitees deemed themselves unworthy and made excuses.[53]

When the Master heard this, He became angry and quickly sent His servants out again to the streets and lanes of the city to bring in the poor and crippled and blind and lame. He told them to invite as many people as they could find.[54]

When the servants reported that it had been done and there was still room, the Master sent them out again to the highways and hedges, to the farthest places that hadn't yet been told of the wedding feast to compel people to come in.[55]

The Master's commands become more and more urgent and more and more far-reaching each time. First, the servants merely inform those who are invited. When the first group of people deemed

---

51   Acts 8:35
52   Acts 6:3-5
53   Matthew 22:1-5; Luke 14:18
54   Matthew 22:9b; Luke 14:21
55   Luke 14:22-23

themselves unworthy of the invitation, the servants' orders were to move on to new people. Then, the servants issued new invitations to an entirely different group of people. After those people accepted, there was still room, so the Master urged the servants to go even farther away to find more people and to compel them to come into the wedding feast.

We need to consider in our day where these highways and hedges might be. Where are those who still have not been told of the coming feast in the age to come? There are literally billions of people living on this earth who have yet to hear that God crucified His Son over 2,000 ago. How is that possible? How has the most excellent news of all time still not reached the ears of every person? Especially when airplanes exist!

America has enjoyed nearly four centuries of access to the Gospel. In that same four centuries, how many unreached human beings have died and gone to Hell without ever hearing about our blessed hope? We are the only stewards of the mysteries of God; if we don't preach, no one will. Seeds don't plant themselves, and foundations do not lay themselves. The Gospel doesn't preach itself. As Christians, it is necessary that we preach the Gospel.

In going to the proverbial "highways and hedges" of our day, we will likely be led to places we don't want to go. There's a reason why the unreached are still unreached after 2 millennia. One contributing factor is that we don't know when to shake the dust of a place off our feet.[56] We need to be asking the question, when do we wipe the dust of this neighborhood or city or country from our feet? When do we acknowledge that people have judged themselves unworthy of eternal life and go on to those who haven't? I believe the Lord will direct us clearly as we ask this question.

> "And Paul and Barnabas spoke out boldly saying, 'It was necessary that the word of God be spoken first to you. Since you thrust it aside and judge yourselves unworthy of eternal life, behold, we are turning to the Gentiles...they shook off the dust from their feet against them and went to Iconium."[57]

---

56   Luke 9:5
57   Acts 13:46,51

LAX

One Christmas, my dad flew me home from New Zealand to be together for the holidays. I landed in the LA airport and had to collect my bags and go through customs before boarding my last flight home. A woman with TSA was rudely shouting orders to everyone funneling into the customs line. While waiting, I heard a man being especially sarcastic and hurtful to his wife. I almost said something to him because I was so frustrated to be around such suffocating negativity. It was unbearable. At that moment, I clearly heard the Lord speak to me, "Jordan, if you preach, I'll make them listen."

What? What do you mean make them listen? Will God shut the mouths and open the ears of these people for me to share the Gospel? No, He couldn't...could He? Again, I clearly felt the urge in my gut to preach to them and that He would cause them to listen. I looked over at the angry TSA lady, and the crowd of people herding into line and became scared. What if they don't listen? What if they are annoyed or I look stupid?

But a third time, I definitely heard the voice of Jesus tell me, "If you preach to them, I will make them listen." But in my heart I knew I wasn't going to. I began justifying my reasons for not obeying. I explained to God why it wasn't a good idea. It was the day before Christmas. If this becomes a security issue, I may be detained and miss the holiday. What would my dad think if he had to call in and vouch for me? Or worse, what if they gave me a full cavity search? Then to my sincere regret, I lowered my head and shuffled my feet, indistinguishable from anyone else in line.

All that to say, I know what it's like to ignore clear promptings from God's Spirit. Unfortunately, I've experienced it many times. It's not the end of the road when we fail to act when God asks us. Just ask Jonah. But we don't want to stay there. We need to repent of our disobedience and ask the Lord to help us act on those promptings in the future. He's faithful, and He's kind. He will do it.

WHAT IS PREVENTING US?

With the stakes so incredibly high in regards to the eternal destinies of human souls, why do we still have so much hesitation about reaching out to other people? In the case that I am not the only one who has found ways to excuse myself from obeying God in preaching the Gospel, let's look at common reasons that prevent many of us from giving a faithful witness.

As strange as this may sound, I find that, often times, fellow Christians can be some of the biggest discouragers of sharing the Gospel. If someone doesn't like your approach or if your frequent preaching convicts him or her, they may offer reasons why they believe you shouldn't do or say this or that. And if we don't feel the support and permission from our own brothers and sisters, we're certainly not going to get it anywhere else in the world. We need to be encouraging to one another in this endeavor, even if our methods or approaches differ.

Weak theology is another culprit in the discouragement of evangelism. It's no wonder to me that when a Christian culture starts believing, for example, that there is no Hell, that they have little concern for people who are going there daily in droves. If we accept the deceitful doctrine of false teachers, it will impair our ability to give a full and faithful witness of the whole counsel of God. In fact, one of the premier responsibilities of an evangelist is to help equip the church for ministry, to build up the body of Christ to attain unity of faith and knowledge of Jesus, so that we may no longer be tossed back and forth by every cunning doctrine.[58] The evangelist should help protect his brothers and sisters from false and dangerous teachings.

Fear is one of the biggest obstacles to evangelism. Whether fear of other's opinions, fear of failure, rejection, or persecution. We can even fear offending other people—even if by accident. It's reasonable to consider these issues. There will be consequences for obedience to Jesus—in this life. And sometimes those consequences will be very severe.

They Hated Jeremiah

Suffering and persecution are a natural part of the Christian life.[59] Just by associating with Jesus, hardships will come our way. Imagine if we were to add boldly preaching a message that the world around us does not want to hear. How much harder will life become for us?

---

58 Ephesians 4:11-14
59 2 Timothy 3:12

Watch what happens to Jeremiah when he says what God is speaking to him and the people don't want to hear it:

> "O Lord, You have deceived me, and I was deceived; You are stronger than I, and You have prevailed. I have become a laughingstock all the day, everyone mocks me. For whenever I speak, I cry out, I shout, 'Violence and destruction!' For the word of the Lord has become for me a reproach and derision all day long. If I say, 'I will not mention Him, or speak any more in His name,' there is in my heart as it were a burning fire shut up in my bones, and I am weary of holding it in, and I cannot."[60]

Jeremiah was not shouting and yelling "destruction" because he was a bitter evangelist tired of seeing no fruit. Jeremiah was being faithful to warn the people as the Lord had directed him. And the people hated him for it. Muslims, atheists, Jews, the LGBT community, the person who rang you up in the checkout lane the last time you bought groceries—literally everyone you've ever encountered anywhere—they all need to know that they are going to stand before God on Judgment Day. They need to know that they need—we want them—to have Christ as their Advocate when they do. But they may very well hate you for delivering that message.

Jesus told us that we would receive similar treatment to what He suffered. On one occasion, Jesus was preaching to men who were enamored with His authority one moment; but in the very next, when He said something they didn't want to hear, they were filled with rage and tried to throw Him off a cliff.[61] When you are giving a faithful witness to the full counsel of God, people may be "filled with rage" and "seek to kill you,"[62] but you must not necessarily assume that you are doing something wrong. You could be doing something wrong, but Jesus was blameless, and these words were uttered against Him. And they tried to *throw Him off a cliff!* We don't have any reason to expect better treatment than Jesus had. He left us an example to follow.

---

60 Jeremiah 20:7-9
61 Luke 4:14-30
62 John 7:1

> "If the world hates you, know that it has hated Me before it hated you. If you were of the world, the world would love you as its own; but because you are not of the world, but I chose you out of the world, therefore the world hates you. Remember the word that I said to you: 'A servant is not greater than his master.' If they persecuted Me, they will also persecute you. If they kept My word, they will also keep yours. But all these things they will do to you on account of My name because they do not know Him who sent Me…I have said all these things to you to keep you from falling away… Indeed, the hour is coming when whoever kills you will think he is offering service to God. And they will do these things because they have not known the Father, nor Me. But I have said these things to you, that when their hour comes you may remember that I told them to you."[63]

They hated Jeremiah, and they hated Jesus. They are going to hate you. It's easy to imagine this happening in the Middle East, but make no mistake, even if you live in the suburbs of America, persecution will find you. We have been promised that.

> "Then they will deliver you up to tribulation and put you to death, and you will be hated by all nations for My name's sake. And then many will fall away and betray one another and hate one another."[64]

But Jesus told us this beforehand so that, when the time came, we would remember and not fall away. And He modeled to us how to entrust our souls to God while enduring great suffering.

> "Therefore let those who suffer according to God's will entrust their souls to a faithful Creator while doing good."[65]

> "For to this, you have been called, because Christ also suffered for you, leaving you an example, so that you might follow in His steps. He committed no sin, neither

---

[63] See John 15:18-16:4
[64] Matthew 24:9-10
[65] 1 Peter 4:19

was deceit found in His mouth. When He was reviled, He did not revile in return; when He suffered, He did not threaten, but continued entrusting Himself to Him who judges justly."[66]

Jesus suffered unjustly, according to God's will, by the hands of men who hated Him. He did not threaten them, but He entrusted Himself to God and left us an example to follow. The crucifixion of Jesus was according to the foreknowledge, and definite planning of God,[67] and God did not intervene. They persecuted Jesus this way, and they will likewise persecute us the same. They hated Him in whom there is no fault. Someone somewhere will surely hate us. Because we aren't only preaching an offensive message—unlike Jesus, we also won't carry it flawlessly (this is not to excuse reprehensible behavior or irresponsible stewardship. But we'll never be perfect).

Sometimes their hatred will ultimately lead to our deaths. But take heart: "Precious in the sight of the Lord is the death of His saints."[68] The Lord is not emotionally disconnected or uninvested in the cost His children must pay to make His name known. But if we are to give a faithful witness of our crucified Messiah, it may come at the dear price of being crucified ourselves. "Rejoice in that day, and leap for joy, for behold, your reward is great in heaven; for so their fathers did to the prophets."[69]

False prophets in Jeremiah's day sound eerily similar to the false teachers in ours. "They say continually, to those who despise the word of the Lord, 'It shall be well with you'; and to everyone who stubbornly follows his own heart, they say, 'No disaster shall come upon you.'"[70] When Christians tell the world what it wants to hear, they will likely be received favorably. But at what cost? If we don't warn their souls, there is blood on our hands. If we want our conscience to be free, we need to bear witness to the whole counsel of God. His kindness and severity. Faithful servants do not pick and choose from the message their Master sent them with. We tell it all, even if it causes the world to hate and despise us.

---

66   1 Peter 2:21-23
67   Acts 2:23
68   Psalm 116:15
69   Luke 6:23
70   Jeremiah 23:17

Sometimes, if we follow the Lamb wherever He goes, it will mean being led like a sheep to the slaughter.[71] But we must remember that it is the excellent leadership of the Good Shepherd bringing us there. "Therefore let those who suffer according to God's will entrust their souls to a faithful Creator while doing good."[72]

"Behold, I am sending you out as sheep in the midst of wolves, so be wise as serpents and innocent as doves."[73] The exhortation to be wise is not a call to avoid wolves, it is a call to be wise while we are in their midst. We need not to run away from the Shepherd, even when He leads us into danger.

You Have Permission

You have permission by God, the Creator and Author of life, to obey Him rather than men.[74] People will tell you that it's not the right time or place or circumstance to share your faith. Well, when is it? When is it a convenient time to hear about the need for a Savior? The souls of men and women are more important than the potential annoyance that you might cause by telling them about Christ. Be considerate, but you don't have to be sorry for caring about people's souls.

And when consequences come, you have permission to rejoice! The Lord's response to threats and persecution is to give more boldness to continue preaching,[75] and affirming His disciples when they suffer.

> "Then they left the presence of the council, rejoicing that they were counted worthy to suffer dishonor for the name."[76]

> "If you are insulted for the name of Christ, you are blessed, because the Spirit of glory and of God rests upon you."[77]

> "Blessed are you when others revile you and persecute you and utter all kinds of evil against you falsely on My account. Rejoice and be glad, for your reward is great in

---

71 Romans 8:36
72 1 Peter 4:19
73 Matthew 10:16
74 Acts 5:27-30
75 Acts 4:29
76 Acts 5:41
77 1 Peter 4:14

heaven, for so they persecuted the prophets who were before you."[78]

"Bless those who persecute you; bless and do not curse them."[79]

"But I say to you, love your enemies and pray for those who persecute you."[80]

"So they called them and charged them not to speak or teach at all in the name of Jesus. But Peter and John answered them, 'Whether it is right in the sight of God to listen to you rather than to God, you must judge, for we cannot but speak of what we have seen and heard.' And when they had further threatened them, they let them go, finding no way to punish them, because of the people, for all were praising God for what had happened."[81]

"And the high priest questioned them, saying, 'We strictly charged you not to teach in this name, yet here you have filled Jerusalem with your teaching, and you intend to bring this Man's blood upon us.' But Peter and the apostles answered, 'We must obey God rather than men.'"[82]

The early church was born into persecution, and yet, they were some of the boldest Christians the world has ever known. I believe that is why Paul's charge to Timothy to do the work of an evangelist included an appeal to "endure suffering."[83] If we want the Gospel to advance and God's church to grow, we must be a people who proclaim what He has done no matter the consequence. This is something I believe the persecuted Church in the Middle East can teach the Church in the West—if we have ears to hear.

---

78 Matthew 5:11-12
79 Romans 12:14
80 Matthew 5:44
81 Acts 4:18-21
82 Acts 5:27-29
83 2 Timothy 4:5

Measurable Multiplication

According to Paul, the work of a good soldier (or a good servant) of Christ is to entrust faithful men with the Gospel:

> "You then, my child, be strengthened by the grace that is in Christ Jesus, and what you have heard from me in the presence of many witnesses entrust to faithful men, who will be able to teach others also."[84]

Paul (generation one) tells Timothy (generation two) entrust to faithful men (generation three) who teach others (generation four). In this one sentence, we see Paul's strategy of making multiple generations of obedient, reproducing disciples.

Paul goes on to encourage Timothy in the work of an evangelist.[85] We know from the fourth chapter of Ephesians what Paul has in mind when he instructs Timothy to do the work of an evangelist. An evangelist (along with apostles, prophets, teachers, and shepherds) is a servant to help the body and help equip laypeople for the work of ministry.[86] Paul isn't merely telling Timothy to share the Gospel; he is also urging Timothy to equip others in the community to share the Gospel as well. Again, we see this strategy in the action of making multiple generations of reproducing disciples. Paul's letter endeavors to instill this strategy in Timothy—and in us.

In his first letter to Timothy, Paul gives a practical appeal that is often left uncultivated in our church-planting and disciple-making methodology. He says, "Practice these things, immerse yourself in them, so that all may see your progress."[87] How often have we felt inclined to practice and track our progress in regards to disciple-making? Paul is teaching that there are good reasons to exercise leadership and disciple-making skills in the sight of others and to track our progress in them together.

It can be very beneficial to gauge our fruitfulness and track our effectiveness in reproducing disciples. Matthew teaches us that Gospel seeds planted in good soil reproduce thirty, sixty, and one-hundred

---

84 2 Timothy 2:1-2
85 2 Timothy 4:5
86 Ephesians 4:11-13
87 1 Timothy 4:15

times.[88] In the same way we have an expectation that planting a tomato seed in good soil would produce many more tomatoes, there is an expectation that planting the Gospel in good soil would produce many more disciples.

> "When they had preached the Gospel to that city and had made many disciples, they returned to Lystra and to Iconium and to Antioch."[89]

When the apostles preached the Gospel, they made many disciples. Being a faithful witness should result in actively making many disciples. If it doesn't, we need to ask the Lord about how we need to adjust humbly, and He will be faithful to show us. We may need to exchange formerly held beliefs or methodologies to obey the call to make disciples more effectively. I'm not saying that it's man's responsibility to save a human soul. Quite the opposite. Only God can do that. But if our approach or method becomes too inflexible, it can really limit our ability to obey the great commission in a way that bears the fruit of reproducing disciples.

> "As for what was sown on good soil, this is the one who hears the word and understands it. He indeed bears fruit and yields, in one case a hundredfold, in another sixty, and in another thirty."[90]

> "As for what was sown among thorns, this is the one who hears the word, but the cares of the world and the deceitfulness of riches choke the word, and it proves unfruitful."[91]

We can be born again believers in Jesus and yet absolutely irrelevant to the Great Commission. If we aren't making disciples, we have to be honest and admit that it could be because the cares of this world are choking the Great Commission out of us. As disciples of Jesus, we should be faithful. And we should be effective.

Our salvation is not at stake if we do not bear fruit in disciple-making.

---

88 Matthew 13:18-23
89 Acts 14:21
90 Matthew 13:23
91 Matthew 13:22

I want to be really clear about that. But we will suffer a significant loss. "If anyone's work is burned up, he will suffer loss, though he himself will be saved, but only as through fire."[92] We will be saved, for sure, but we may have to watch our entire life's work go up in flames because we spent our days building that which is eternally insignificant.

> "According to the grace of God given to me, like a skilled master builder I laid a foundation, and someone else is building upon it. Let each one take care how he builds upon it. For no one can lay a foundation other than that which is laid, which is Jesus Christ. Now if anyone builds on the foundation with gold, silver, precious stones, wood, hay, straw—each one's work will become manifest, for the Day will disclose it, because it will be revealed by fire, and the fire will test what sort of work each one has done."[93]

I'm not just talking about worldly pursuits or career choices. Twenty years among unreached people groups could be considered of no lasting, eternal value to Jesus because we focused solely on relieving temporal human suffering without any regard to the eternal souls in our care. If we heal every wound in Iraq and Syria but do not share the good news that saves souls, will that work survive when tested?

These lessons learned from Paul include many actionable points that can really serve to ground and shape our disciple-making efforts today. If we heed them, I believe it will bring strength to our work as servants sent by the Master.

Closing

There are mysteries of God that have been hidden for ages[94] which previous generations have inquired about but were not permitted to know. Angels too have longed to look into them but were not able. But to us, the people of God, it has now been revealed.[95]

> "The mystery hidden for ages and generations but now revealed to His saints. To them, God chose to make known

---

92 1 Corinthians 3:15
93 1 Corinthians 3:10-13
94 Ephesians 3:4-5
95 1 Peter 1:10-12

how great among the Gentiles are the riches of the glory of this mystery, which is—Christ in you—the hope of glory. Him we proclaim, warning everyone and teaching everyone."[96]

What an exclusive privilege! Of all creatures in the universe, only people can comprehend these mysteries. And of all people who have ever existed, only those after Christ may fully know them. And of those after Christ who can recognize them, only His followers actually do. And of all Christ's followers who see this mystery, how many of us indeed proclaim it?

The unspeakable joy of this revelation was not given to us for us alone. It's for us and for those who do not yet know Him. "I do not ask for these only, but also for those who will believe in My through their word."[97] Jesus voiced this desire when He said, "I have other sheep that are not of this fold. I must bring them also, and they will listen to My voice."[98] It's our responsibility to tell them.[99] It is required of us, as God's fellow workers,[100] that we are found diligently working in His field, planting and watering as God has assigned us. The Lord's concern for shepherdless people and His urgency to have them as His own far outweighs the light momentary afflictions we will face on His account. Jesus' name is worth whatever it costs to tell those who have not yet heard about Him.

An Original Poem

There is a Day approaching, His holy name attached;
The more come to Him now, the fewer feel His wrath.
Our commission then is clear, we know what we're to do;
Give ourselves to Jesus' will, until others know Him too.
From every tribe, from every tongue, His worshippers will be;
God is committed to this end, but I ask, are you and me?
Let us then adore Him, until aligned are we;
Jesus' dream is supreme, do our lives agree?

---

96 Colossians 1:26-28
97 John 17:20
98 John 10:16
99 Romans 10:14-15
100 1 Corinthians 3:8-9

SECTION III

THE JOY OF MAKING DISCIPLES

> *"And those servants went out into the roads an gathered all whom they found, both bad and good. So the wedding hall was filled with guests."*[1]

This passage is excellent news for the servants of Christ. Our mission will succeed. The Master's house will be filled. We know from Revelation chapter seven that this wedding feast will actually take place in the age to come and that it will be filled with guests.

> "After this I looked, and behold, a great multitude that no one could number, from every nation, from all tribes and peoples and languages, standing before the throne and before the Lamb, clothed in white robes, with palm branches in their hands, and crying out with a loud voice, 'Salvation belongs to our God who sits on the throne, and to the Lamb!'"[2]

The wedding hall will be filled with people from every ethnically

---

[1] Matthew 22:10
[2] Revelation 7:9-10

distinct people group on earth, worshipping Jesus forever in the age to come! And the Master wants us to go out and bring them in now.

Have you ever wondered why? *Why* would God prefer to use humans to make His appeal to the lost to be reconciled to God? Wouldn't it be more useful for Him to use more reliable means? After all, in the last chapter, we identified several obstacles that so often keep us back from being faithful witnesses.

God is looking for more worshippers, but He's also much more concerned with the joy and maturity of those who are already in His family. Working *with* His *existing* disciples to being in those who are *not-yet* disciples is one of Jesus' most excellent strategies for cultivating our maturity and dependence on Him. As we've seen, this task is not one that can be done effectively apart from a dynamic relationship with God. By taking our responsibility to the lost seriously, God is maturing us into the likeness of His Son. It's for our good, and working with Him is enjoyable!

OBEDIENCE IS LOVE

Not enjoying God is the principal reason why Christians do not evangelize. Let me explain what I mean by that. Could you imagine praising something you didn't enjoy? Or advertising a product that you don't believe in? Would you recommend a restaurant if you didn't like their food? Of course not!! Likewise, if we don't enjoy God, we will not praise Him before others. If anyone received mercy but does not propagate that mercy, there is a severe deficiency in their understanding.

God's Plan A for securing more souls is praise. Praise is everywhere. It is the most common response to enjoying something. In fact, it's abnormal not to praise things. C.S. Lewis had a lot of clarity on this issue:

> "I think we delight to praise what we enjoy because the praise not merely expresses but completes the enjoyment; it is its appointed consummation. It is not out of compliment that lovers keep on telling one another how beautiful they are; the delight is incomplete till it is expressed. It is frustrating to have discovered a new author and not to be able to tell anyone how good he is; to come suddenly,

at the turn of the road, upon some mountain valley of unexpected grandeur and then to have to keep silent because the people with you care for it no more than for a tin can in the ditch; to hear a good joke and find no one to share it with. . . .The Scotch catechism says that man's chief end is 'to glorify God and enjoy Him forever.' But we shall then know that these are the same thing. Fully to enjoy is to glorify. In commanding us to glorify Him, God is inviting us to enjoy Him."[3]

Writing for Desiring God, Sam Storms expanded on Lewis' thoughts from above:

"So, Lewis is telling us that God's pursuit of our praise of Him is not weak self-seeking but the epitome of self-giving love! If our satisfaction in God is incomplete until expressed in praise of Him for satisfying us with Himself (note well, with Himself, not His gifts), then God's effort to elicit my worship (what Lewis before thought was inexcusable selfishness) is both the most loving thing He could possibly do for me and the most glorifying thing He could possibly do for Himself."[4]

So, if we aren't praising Jesus to other people, it would be fair to question whether we are genuinely enjoying Him at all. Because when we treasure Jesus more than life, it's normal that we would speak of Him to others.

I often use the analogy of a reflex test to help describe how I see evangelism. When you're up on the examination table, and the doctor hits his little rubber hammer just under your kneecap, your leg will kick. It's the natural response of a healthy reflex. But if you purposefully tense your muscles when the hammer strikes, your leg will not kick. Likewise, when a human heart finds pleasure in God, the most natural response is to praise Him, to talk about Him, to discuss Him. But often, we tense up and instead withhold our most natural and healthy response.

---

3   Lewis, C.S. (1958) *Reflections on the Psalms*. Harcourt, Brace.
4   Storms, Sam (2013) Praise: The Consummation of Joy. Retrived from https://www.desiringgod.org/articles/praise-the-consummation-of-joy

What are we to do when we are found refraining from praising God to others? How do we enjoy Jesus so much that our natural response is to praise Him? I believe obedience is how that happens.

> "If you keep My commands, you will remain in My love, just as I have kept My Father's commandments and abide in His love. These things I have spoken to you, that My joy may be in you and that your joy may be full."[5]

John, the disciple whom Jesus loved, understood that obeying Jesus is loving Jesus. Jesus Himself said, "If you love me, you will keep My commandments."[6] The reason Jesus gives for wanting us to obey Him is so that His joy may be in us and that our joy may be full! Obedience to Jesus is how we express our love to Him. Fortunately for us, it results in our satisfaction. What do we seek in life, if not to be satisfied?

But enjoying God doesn't just happen because we embrace a view of Him that says He's enjoyable. Obeying Him is how we enjoy Him. And of course, I absolutely mean following Him in every way, but most specifically, I mean obeying His commission to make disciples. Let me explain why:

It is exhilarating to watch a person begin to see the glory of God in the face of Jesus, especially when you are the one who facilitated the experience. It's addicting. You feel the partnership of God and the wind of heaven on your back, the blessing of the Lord each time you breathe. It is invigorating to participate in God's process of making disciples of Jesus.

It's such a life-giving and exciting experience because we're not merely going to invite people to a wedding reception in this age, but into what we have; into the joys of belonging to God, being enjoyed by Jesus, and knowing the pleasure of worshipping Him. We're going to call men and women into their calling so that they too can preach Christ to people who don't know Him. We're not going out merely to talk with others. We're going to introduce the world to Christ in us; the hope of glory. It's such a joyful thing.

Obeying God in every way is life-giving. But I think there is a special

---

5   John 15:10-11
6   John 14:15

blessing of joy and maturity in the Lord when we follow His call to make disciples in every nation. When we agree with God that His name will be celebrated in all the earth, we're putting stakes in ground that belongs to us. We're making it clear that we won't let the rocks have our inheritance—we will cry out ourselves, in love![7]

Here's a quick thought to help keep our focus on the Savior: if our response to the free gift of salvation is to applaud our own choice in the process, we might be doing it wrong. It was a gift "so that no one may boast."[8] And it's to the praise of His glory,[9] not to the praise of our response. Reminding ourselves of this will help us maintain a healthy expectation for God to be the decisive factor in someone coming to the Lord.

SONG OF SOLOMON

Quite possibly, the happiest moment of my life was one of the first times I shared the Gospel. My heart was so full I felt like I could either blow up or float away or maybe both. I walked across the street to rejoin my friends after sharing with a stranger, feeling like I was twelve feet tall and indestructible!

I feel the delight of God when I talk about Him to others. In almost every occasion that I go out with a group to evangelize, nearly every single person comes back with a fresh glow on their face and happiness in their soul. Human beings love to praise what they love. Just ask one of your friends who fell in love recently. Look up at a billboard advertising a product. Listen to the conversations at a restaurant. Praise is all around us. It is the primary way we communicate what we enjoy.

The Song of Solomon, believe it or not, has one of my favorite depictions of evangelism in the whole Bible. A large part of the book is following a woman who is continually praising her beloved to others. There is so much we can gain from watching how people respond to her praise. In the first chapter, she declares, "Your love is better than wine."[10]

Others in her midst affirm her statement saying, "We will exult and

---

7   Luke 19:40
8   Ephesians 2:9
9   Ephesians 1:6,12,14
10 Song of Solomon 1:2

rejoice in you; we will extol your love more than wine; rightly do they love you."[11]

What would it be like for people to praise God more than they appreciate beer and wine or sports? I am not opposed to celebrating remarkable sports plays and victories, but I am saying that if men were to praise God the same way we praise sports, perhaps the unbeliever would find Him all the more attractive. Advertising works because praise is a foolproof method for attracting people to something.

"What is your beloved more than another beloved...that you thus adjure us?"[12] What is so special about this God that you would plead with us to see Him? The woman, wounded by the absence of her beloved, begins to speak a very impassioned list of His attributes to those listening:

> "My beloved is radiant and ruddy, distinguished among then thousand...he is altogether desirable. This is my beloved and this is my friend, O daughters of Jerusalem."[13]

And at the end of her discourse, the people she was talking with responded,

> "Where has your beloved gone...where has your beloved turned that we may seek him with you?"[14]

The praise of Jesus makes others desire Him too. May that be the response of those around us when we sing the praises of the One our soul loves!

MARY

There is an account in Scripture of a woman who poured costly perfume over the head and feet of Jesus. Mary of Bethany, as she is known, treasured Jesus far more than a considerable sum of money. Jesus called what she had done "a beautiful thing."[15] That young girl saw something in Jesus that even His closest followers neglected to see; the high value of God in the flesh that far surpassed anything of

---

11 Song of Solomon 1:4
12 Song of Solomon 5:9
13 Song of Solomon 5:10-16
14 Song of Solomon 6:1
15 Matthew 26:10

measurable worth. Jesus, moved by this act, commanded that "wherever the Gospel is proclaimed in the whole world, what she has done will be told in memory of her."[16] If Jesus put such high value in what Mary had done, I think it would be very wise for us to model our lives after her example and be found enjoying God to such a high degree.

> "And while He was at Bethany in the house of Simon, the leper, as He was reclining at table, a woman came with an alabaster flask of ointment of pure nard, very costly, and she broke the flask and poured it over His head. Some said to themselves indignantly, 'Why was the ointment wasted like that? For this ointment could have been sold for more than three hundred denarii and given to the poor.' And they scolded her. But Jesus said, 'Leave her alone. Why do you trouble her? She has done a beautiful thing for Me. For you always have the poor with you, and whenever you want, you can do good for them. But you will not always have Me. She has done what she could; she has anointed My body beforehand for burial. And truly, I say to you, wherever the Gospel is proclaimed in the whole world, what she has done will be told in memory of her.'"[17]

What stands out to me is that this account of Mary valuing Jesus above everything else ends with a commission to tell others. The joy this woman found in Jesus is meant to be spread to others all over the world. There is joy in the heart of God whenever a sinner repents. It is no dull day in heaven when a person's soul is saved.[18] God enjoys pardoning sinners; He is delighted to it![19]

Are you glad to be saved? So would others be if only they knew who you know? Let's contribute to the joy in heaven by helping lead men and women to the saving knowledge of the Son of God. And let's help them find all they have ever wanted in Him.

DAVID

Many prophets in Jewish history exult in God with gladness, but

---

16 Matthew 26:13
17 Mark 14:3-9
18 Luke 15:10
19 Micah 7:18

none more pronounced than King David. Here was a man who was not afraid to let the world know that he enjoyed God, dancing before the Lord with all his might.[20] In Psalm 103, David tells us, "Forget not all His benefits." King David reminded himself of the benefits of belonging to God, and it served him as a fuel for worship.

May we also not forget all of His benefits. The Lord forgives all our iniquity and heals all our diseases.[21] Our lives are redeemed from the pit, and we are crowned with enduring love and mercy.[22] God satisfies us with good and gives justice to all who are oppressed.[23] He does not deal with us according to our iniquities.[24] Jesus' love toward those who fear Him is as high as the heavens.[25] He removes our transgressions permanently[26] and is compassionate towards us in our frailty.[27]

Because of all these things, David, being in awe of God's character, demands that the angels bless the Lord, and commands his own soul to follow suit.[28] Below are verses I find helpful when appealing to someone beyond what he or she will be saved from, but by what they will have access to in Christ. Being saved does refer to escaping Hell, but it is so much more than that!

> "But to all who did receive Him, who believed in His name, He gave the right to become children of God, who were born, not of blood nor of the will of the flesh nor of the will of man, but of God."[29]

In the Psalms, David says that because God's love is better than life, his lips will praise Him.[30] And in God's presence, there is the fullness of joy and pleasures forever.[31] By knowing what pleasures we have access to now, and the pleasures that await us in the next age, we can

---

20   2 Samuel 6:14
21   Psalm 103:3
22   Psalm 103:4
23   Psalm 103:5-6
24   Psalm 103:10
25   Psalm 103:11
26   Psalm 103:12
27   Psalm 103:13-14
28   Psalm 103:20-22
29   John 1:12
30   Psalm 63:3-4
31   Psalm 16:11

help our pleasure-seeking generation[32] forsake their broken cisterns[33] and their hollow pursuit of empty pleasures that do not satisfy so they can take without cost the satisfaction in God which truly will satisfy them eternally.[34]

Mankind wants to be happy, and God provides the ultimate happiness in Himself. In his book *When I Don't Desire God*, John Piper addresses the elusive happiness that man seeks and presents us with abiding happiness found in Christ:

> "The object of our wants is ultimately a psychological experience of happiness without any regard to what makes us happy. In other words...the final object of our pursuit is joy itself, rather than the beauty of what we find joy in. This is a very common mistake."[35]

We need to show people that happiness apart from God will always be temporary, it will forever evade them, and they will never be satisfied until they say, with Piper, "I want to know the One, and the only One, who is in Himself all I have ever longed for in all my desires to be happy."[36]

God has invited all mankind to receive adoption as sons and be grafted into His covenants with the patriarchs. To be included in this covenants is to be the recipient of God's promises. We will have no tears, no pain, and no injustice for eternity in paradise.[37] Confident access to the throne of grace now[38] and friendship with God who made everything.[39] We have a purpose.[40] We have obtained freedom from the devil's hold, from oppression and lies. We are no longer slaves to sin and Satan because his power has been defeated.[41] We will be presented blameless before the presence of God's glory with great

---

32 2 Timothy 3:4
33 Jeremiah 2:13
34 Isaiah 55:1-2
35 Piper, John (2004) *When I Don't Desire God: How to Fight for Joy*. Wheaton, IL: Crossway Books.
36 Ibid.
37 Revelation 21:4
38 Ephesians 3:12; Hebrews 4:16;10:19
39 Proverbs 22:11; John 15:15
40 Ephesians 2:10
41 Colossians 2:13-15

joy.[42] And now, for those who come to Christ, one of the phrases that unbelievers have previously used to comfort themselves will actually be true for them: Peace on earth among men with whom God is pleased.[43] God will work all things for good for those who love Him and are called *according to His purpose*.[44]

Getting Practical

Not everyone will emulate Paul in the sense of following His missionary endeavors by traveling around the globe. Some people will be more like Stephen and Phillip and live faithful lives in their own communities, and it's important that we realize having a "normal" job is one of the most productive ways to make disciples. Working laypeople in the Church already have built years of acquaintanceship with multiple people they see every day. Not much needs to change in a person's daily life to have a substantial impact on the Great Commission right where they are.

Think about it: you already know the culture. You already speak the language. You already have a rapport with the people. Your home is established and ready for hosting your lost neighbors. Your children make friends that lead you to meet their parents. School, work, soccer games, the gym, coffee shops, gas stations. Every place you go daily without interrupting your rhythm and routine is full of opportunities to disciple the lost.

And this is all for the sake of fuller joy in God. As I mentioned, adopting a view of God as enjoyable doesn't necessarily result in enjoying God more. Seeing Him, savoring Him, enjoying Him in prayer are all necessary to that end, but I'm willing to bet that our enjoyment will be limited if there is a lack of disciple-making in our lives. When we experience firsthand the joys of helping another person see Him and fall in love with Him, then we will understand the exhilaration that comes from obeying Jesus and will have the confidence to expect the disciples we are making to do the same!

For the Joy Set Before Him

The most apparent revelation we have of God the Father is in the

---

42   Jude 1:24-25
43   Luke 2:14
44   Romans 8:28

face of Jesus Christ. "He is the radiance of the glory of God and the exact imprint of His nature."[45] God says of His Son, "Therefore God, your God, has anointed You with the oil of gladness beyond Your companions.[46] So when we look at the most potent representation of the nature of God, we see the happiest Man in the world.

Since God is the source of rivers of delight,[47] it is safe to say that he is not a sad God. He made the world and everything in it and is not served by human hands.[48] God needs nothing from us and is completely happy in Himself. The happiness of God is clearly expressed in the way He relates to His Son. God publicly spoke from heaven to affirm Jesus as His beloved Son in whom He is well pleased.[49] The Holy Spirit of God rests with the Son of God and God the Father is pleased with Him. Luke records Jesus rejoicing in the Holy Spirit and thanking His Father for His good pleasure in revealing mysteries to the disciples.[50] By these examples, we are given insight into the enjoyment God has had since before the word existed.[51] I think the point is sufficiently made that God is happy in Himself.

And since God needs nothing, it is quite remarkable to note that God made men, not out of deficiency, but out of surplus, as an overflow of His infinite reservoir of selfless love. And Jesus, with the most beautiful prayer ever uttered, asked the Father to fulfill the joy They share together in the lives of His disciples.[52]

"I do not ask for these only, but also for those who will believe in Me through their word, that they may all be one, just as You, Father, are in Me, and I in You, that they also may be in Us, so that the world may believe that You have sent Me. The glory that You have given Me I have given to them, that they may be one even as We are one, I in them and You in Me, that they may become perfectly one, so that

---

45 Hebrews 1:3
46 Psalm 45; Hebrews 1:8-9
47 Psalm 36:8
48 Acts 17:24-25
49 See Jesus' baptism in Matthew 3 and transfiguration in Matthew 17. See also Mark 1:11; 9:7; Luke 3:22; 9:35; Peter 1:16-18
50 Luke 10:21
51 John 17:5
52 John 17:13

the world may know that You sent Me and loved them even as You loved Me."[53]

The Son of God requested that we partake in His oneness with the Father so that the world may believe that God sent Him. This is a constant theme throughout Scripture: that the followers of Christ spend time with Jesus and that their time spent together would result in the world hearing about Him through their word.

It pleased the Lord the crush His Son.[54] That is by far the most amazing and refreshing statement I have ever read concerning the crucifixion of Jesus. God was glad to die in your place so that He can enjoy you forever. When has atheism ever suffered and died in your stead? When has any pleasure life has to offer become a sacrifice for us? What else in existence has drunk the dregs of the wrath we deserve so that we could enjoy His fellowship forever? God alone, revealed in Christ, is like this.

As we've already discussed, Jesus was in the garden of Gethsemane sweating blood in agony, greatly distressed because of the cup He was given to drink.[55] And what He says as He stares into that proverbial cup is astounding: "Now is My soul troubled. And what shall I say? 'Father, save Me from this hour'? But for this purpose, I have come to this hour. Father, glorify Your name." Then a voice came from Heaven: "I have glorified it, and I will glorify it again."[56]

He went through with it! Jesus went willingly to the cross. And the book of Hebrews says it was because of "the joy set before Him" that He endured it.[57] Jesus suffered excruciating pain at that time for the sake of joy in the age to come: His joy and ours—to give us access to His joy with Him, forever.

From the place of complete enjoyment in God, we will sing about His greatness and shout His praises to others. What we love about Jesus in prayer, we will loudly proclaim to those who don't know Him. "What I tell you in the dark, say in the light, and what you hear

---

53 John 17:20-23
54 Isaiah 53:10, NASB
55 Matthew 26:39
56 John 12:27-28
57 Hebrews 12:2

whispered, proclaim on the housetops."[58] God's happy with us. When we believe this, we are delighted in God. The lost must be brought into this excellent delight with the Father. If we enjoy belonging to Him, so will they!

TREASURE

There is a reason why the man Matthew tells us about who found a treasure in a field decided to sell everything he had to buy that field joyfully: because the treasure brought him more pleasure than anything else ever could. Jesus is that treasure.

> "The kingdom of heaven is like treasure in a field, which a man found and covered up. Then in his joy he goes and sells all that he has and buys that field."[59]

Jesus is the treasure, and it is our joy to forsake anything that would restrict us from having Him! Recently, I had the incredible privilege of meeting with persecuted believers from the underground Church in Iran. Never have I had such a humbling and inspiring experience. We sat in the same room with men and women from the Muslim world who quite literally sold everything to lay hold of this treasure, and now daily they risk their lives to proclaim Him to others.

You may be aware of the hostile response most former Muslims are met with when they profess their love for Christ. These men and women are no exception. But every single one of them is so madly in love with their Messiah—this Jesus who rescued them—that they will gladly face any opposition on His account. They are the most happy-to-be-saved Christians I have ever met!

We asked one of the men how he has postured his heart in light of the considerable risk and threat of persecution. He told us that he simply keeps all of his hope on the age to come. "What is fifty years in prison compared to eternity with Jesus?"[60]

> "Therefore, preparing your minds for action, and being

---

58 Matthew 10:27
59 Matthew 13:44
60 This interview is included in *Sheep Among Wolves, Vols. I & II* from FAI STUDIOS, free online and in the FAI app.

> sober-minded, set your hope fully on the grace that will be brought to you at the revelation of Jesus Christ."[61]
>
> "Though you have not seen Him, you love Him. Though you do not now see Him, you believe in Him and rejoice with joy that is inexpressible and filled with glory, obtaining the outcome of your faith, the salvation of your souls."[62]

There is a joy in salvation, embedded deeply in our souls, that is inexpressible and filled with glory. Iranian believers know this well. How many more people will experience this joy simply because we opened our mouth and told them about our Lord?

THE HOUSEHOLD OF GOD AND ITS FOUNDATIONS

There is only one foundation on which we can build, and no one can lay another.[63] In his letter to the Church in Ephesus, Paul expounds on the foundation that we are building on. The household of God is not a New Testament idea. It's built on the foundation of the Jewish patriarchs and prophets.[64] We ought to familiarize ourselves with what the apostles and prophets have said concerning this foundation and the people of God because the identity of the Church is bound to the history of the Jewish people.

> "Salvation is from the Jews."[65]
>
> "The Jews were entrusted with the oracles of God."[66]
>
> "They are Israelites, and to them belong the adoption, the glory, the covenants, the giving of the law, the worship, and the promises. To them belong the patriarchs, and from their race, according to the flesh, is the Christ, who is God."[67]
>
> "Therefore remember that you [Gentiles] were at that time separated from Christ, alienated from the commonwealth

---

61 1 Peter 1:13
62 1 Peter 1:8-9
63 1 Corinthians 3:11
64 Ephesians 2:19-20
65 John 4:22
66 Romans 3:2
67 Romans 9:4-5

of Israel and strangers to the covenants of promise, having no hope and without God in world."[68]

Gentiles were formerly strangers to the New Covenant. Isaiah prophesied that God would make a "new covenant" with "those in Jacob."[69] Without ambiguity, Jeremiah foretold that the Lord would "make a new covenant with the house of Israel."[70] An "everlasting covenant" where God will plant Israel in the Land He promised to Abraham with all His heart and soul.[71] Ezekiel agrees with the other prophets in saying that the Lord will be God to the house of Israel.[72] Each mention of the New Covenant is consistent and explicit. In all four accounts, we are shown a new and everlasting covenant with the house of Israel.

> "But now in Christ Jesus, you who once were far off have been brought near by the blood of Christ."[73]

> "When you read this, you can perceive my insight into the mystery of Christ...this mystery is that the Gentiles are fellow heirs, members of the same body, and partakers of the promise in Christ Jesus through the Gospel."[74]

We have been given the incredible privilege of becoming "partakers of the promises." Through Jesus, we are no longer strangers to the covenants. Though we bring nothing to the table, we are permitted to enjoy all the benefits of God's everlasting covenant with Israel.

> "So then you are no longer strangers and aliens, but you are fellow citizens with the saints and members of the household of God."[75]

The foundations of the household of God are thoroughly Jewish. The covenantal promises made to the Jewish patriarchs and prophets, mediated by the Jewish Messiah, and proclaimed by the Jewish

---

68 Ephesians 2:11-12
69 Isaiah 59:20-21
70 Jeremiah 31:31-33
71 Jeremiah 32:40-41
72 Ezekiel 36:24-28
73 Ephesians 2:13
74 Ephesians 3:4-6
75 Ephesians 2:19

apostles are the foundation that the New Testament Church is built on.

Why is this issue so crucial to our work of evangelism and disciple-making? Because any church we plant that is separated from this foundation is no church at all. They are still without hope and without the God of Abraham in the world.

Planting Disciples

At this point, if you're still reading this book, it's safe to assume you have a level of interest in participating in the Great Commission and discipling the lost. But what about for those of us who have families and full-time jobs? How does this affect people who don't have the luxury of ministering as a full-time occupation? How can the rest of us participate in planting reproducing churches?

If we aim to plant churches, we might never end up disciplining the lost. If we seek to disciple the lost, we just might end up planting churches.

There is a lot of preparation that must take place before planting a modern Church is possible. Churches in our day require substantial capital, large buildings, and paid staff on the front end, before even beginning to reach out and disciple new believers. Which means, necessarily, that the primary focus is on securing funding, locating a building, and hiring staff. This approach severely limits the number of those who can plant numerous churches. But what if we took our cues from the early church? Perhaps we might be able to multiply our church planting efforts so dramatically that they actually reflect what we read about in the Word.

In bold contrast to our current model, discipling the lost focuses on just that; discipling the lost. When we enter a new place, we focus on finding those "persons of peace," Jesus referred to in Luke chapter ten. We focus on discipling many to Christ and equipping them as leaders of the Church as it's being formed. Then, when the community is ready, they can decide how to go about acquiring a building space, if that's what they desire. Until that time, we simply meet in homes or at work or in public places like coffee shops or libraries. That way, there is absolutely no cost in forming a group of disciples who will later become leaders of the churches they plant.

I admit my own propensity to write this off as too idealistic to work, but movements across the globe are proving otherwise. It's not wishful thinking. In fact, i's what is modeled to us in God's Word and experienced by tremendously successful disciple-making networks in persecuted nations across Asia and the Middle East today.

Skepticism about making disciples who plant multiple generations of reproducing churches exposes that we don't really believe it's possible to plant churches as frequently as the early disciples did. We err by looking to our own models in modern history and concluding that the explosive church growth we read about in Acts is no longer available to us now. But we should consider the possibility our strategies are clouding our interpretation of Scripture. We could just do what they did in Scripture. It still works.

The modern church planting model employed in the West requires professionals. But simply making disciples can be done with laypeople. Current church planting models focus on buildings and budgets. Disciple-making simply focuses on people. Church planting models often demand a "come and see" approach to evangelism to ensure the seats they just purchased are filled. Disciple-making models require a "go and find" approach that emphasizes reaching people where they're at geographically and forming church communities naturally where the new disciples live and work.

One of the great benefits of facilitating layperson-led disciple-making is fuller engagement from church members. Think about it: churches in the West talk about wanting better participation from their congregations. They preach sermons about not merely being a spectator but really getting involved. But many churches aren't providing an avenue for their members to be involved, especially in planting churches and discipling the lost.

> "He gave the apostles, the prophets, the evangelists, the shepherds, and teachers, to equip the saints for the work of ministry, for building up the body of Christ."[76]

Evangelism and disciple-making are the roles of every Christian. Church leaders are there to equip the saints for the work of this ministry. But the ministry is done by all the saints, not the leaders

---
76 Ephesians 4:11-12

alone. Layperson-led disciple-making is messy, but it's beautiful and effective.[77] And it's fun!

If we start church planting by securing a building first, we're likely to end up with mostly transferred growth from other churches and possibly a few of the new members' unsaved friends. But if we start by disciple-making first, we'll end up with a church comprised of new disciples led by leaders who we have trained and equipped for the task. Approaching church planting this way creates space for everyone to be a church planter. If we're all approved and entrusted with the gospel, and we all have areas of influence, we can plant churches. It's as simple as that.

So instead of planting a church building, what if we simply planted disciples? Disciples who obey Jesus and have a clear mission will be able to produce exponentially more growth than a single building and a paid staff ever could. Let's plant disciples.

SPHERES

While we're on the subject of the expansion of the Church, we should make a couple of things clear. There's a trendy idea going around lately that renewing culture and advancing the gospel of the Kingdom are inherently the same thing. They aren't. Jesus didn't expect or command His disciples to renew the culture or reform society. He expected and commanded us to "make disciples."[78] We should absolutely engage the spheres of influence in society—because that's where people are. But we don't engage social or cultural spheres because we expect the spheres themselves to change the people within them.

We don't need to commandeer the spheres of influence to effectively disciple the men and women in them. Sphere-change may be a result of good discipling, but it certainly is not the goal. We should follow the lead of Jesus and the early church, and keep first things first.

This sphere-centric perspective can creep into the church when we misinterpret the hour we are living in. Some people believe that the conditions on earth are gradually improving until the day all things are perfected. But this couldn't be farther from what Scripture teaches about what's to come. We have ironclad promises that things are

---

77   Proverbs 14:4
78   Matthew 28:19

going to get worse and worse as the Day of the Lord draws closer.[79] Let's not waste our energies attempting to thwart those promises by demanding the godless culture around us to change. Instead, let's disciple the lost—personally and effectively.

The kingdom of God is not an ethereal kingdom. It's not merely a metaphor for God's authority and sovereignty in this age. It is a literal, physical kingdom that will reside on the face of the earth in the age to come. And that kingdom has a king. The king of Kings. Jesus will literally, physically, bodily return and rule from actual Jerusalem. So when we're talking about advancing the gospel of the Kingdom, we're not suggesting that we are gaining physical ground for the King in this age. Don't get me wrong, we are excited when people of this age begin to obey the King, and it necessarily affects their spheres of influence. But we need to be careful not to confuse that with expanding the physical kingdom of God. That will happen. But it will happen when Jesus returns to do it Himself. Not before then.

The Theatrical Ambassador

As I've mentioned, I really like the parable of the wedding feast. It has impacted my life and shaped the way I share the gospel with the lost. I've loved this parable since the first time I heard it, from the very beginning of my walk with the Lord. I like it so much that I have literally created gospel tracts to look like wedding invitations to the Marriage Supper of the Lamb, hand-sealed with red wax. I'm really into it.

One day, I was especially excited about it. I had spent the morning in corporate devotional prayer and was reflecting on the parable and getting amped up about the reality it represents. I almost couldn't believe the incredible privilege we've been given to be ambassadors of the coming Kingdom. That morning, I wrote a little play in my journal, letting my theatrical side show a little.

After a while, I couldn't contain myself to the paper. I had to try it out in the real world. And I did. Later that day, when we were doing evangelistic outreach in the community, I walked up to a group of ladies having coffee outside of a mall. I put on my performance voice and

---

[79] For resources regarding Scripture's descriptions of the return of the Messiah, please refer to the synoptic accounts of the Olivet discourse. Additionally, the Maranatha Global Bible Studies are available for free in the FAI app.

began to act out my play about the King, who offered His subjects pardon for their crimes against Him. I didn't get very far before the ladies interjected their thoughts on the subject. I got a little flustered and switched back to my normal voice.

The ladies had a problem with being accused of guilt. I said that the King was willing to forgive them for everything they had ever done in their lives independent from God's loving oversight. I told them it was a severe offense to ignore the leadership of our unfathomably merciful Creator, but that nevertheless, He was eager to forgive them. My emphasis was not on what they did wrong, it was on the willingness of God to forgive them. Still, they could not bring themselves to agree that they were guilty of any such offense.

It really went downhill from there. I tried to focus more exclusively on the character of Jesus and what He's like toward them. But they became annoyed and quickly paid their bill and left. But I didn't feel like it was much of a fruitful conversation, and I was eager to continue talking. I turned to another family that was sitting nearby, watching the whole thing, and I told the father that all the excellent news I was sharing applied to him as well.

That man stood up so fast that his chair tipped over and slid backward. He had just taken a bite of whatever he was eating so as he began to yell at me, little bits of food came tumbling out of his mouth. He screamed expletives at me so loudly that it caused a pretty significant disruption at the cafe. After a nearby janitor saw me and reported me to security, a guard came to escort me off the premises. I told him that my emphasis was on the goodness of God toward people and that I wasn't aiming to be disruptive or cause a scene. He didn't care. I left a few minutes later.

I tell that story because, even though this particular event didn't stay very light-hearted, I had set out to have some fun with the good news. It's a serious thing to be sure, but God has an unmatched sense of humor, and it just felt right to be a little playful. I think the Good News always requires reverence, but I believe that reverence doesn't always have to be somber. There is a happy reverence for God as well. Also, my friend Caleb will really appreciate that this made it into the book. He gets a kick out of that story.

Another thing I learned from this encounter was that even when we focus on the goodness of God to forgive, and present the news in a light-hearted way, people will still hate Jesus and they will still hate us. Because, as I learned from those ladies, no one likes having their guilt exposed if they don't trust that the One exposing it is for them.

> "But all these things they will do to you on account of My name because they do not know Him who sent Me. If I had not come and spoken to them, they would not have been guilty of sin, but now they have no excuse for their sin."[80]

A Faithful Servant's Reward

Often we think of Jesus' atoning work on the cross as motivation for obedience—which is beautiful. But how often do we look toward His rewards to drive us forward? "An athlete is not crowned unless he competes according to the rules."[81] If we compete according to the rules, we will be crowned! I think it would do the Body of Christ a lot of good to look toward His rewards as a motivator for being faithful witnesses now.

> "The laborer deserves his wages."[82]

> "And remain in the same house, eating and drinking what they provide, for the laborer deserves his wages. Do not go from house to house."[83]

> "He who plants and he who waters are one, and each will receive his wages according to his labor. For we are God's fellow workers. You are God's field, God's building."[84]

As laborers in the Great Commission, we deserve our wages. And we will receive wages proportionate to our labor. This is an exciting inspiration for hard work as a disciple maker. Paul sheds more light on the matter of rewards in his first letter to the Corinthians:

---

80 John 15:21-22
81 2 Timothy 2:5
82 1 Timothy 5:18
83 Luke 10:7
84 1 Corinthians 3:8-9

> "If the work that anyone has built on the foundation survives, he will receive a reward."[85]

Only work that survives the fire will be rewarded. That is a huge motivation to make sure that what we are giving ourselves to is something that Jesus actually wants. Because if our work survives, we will hear the affirmation from our Father in heaven. There's nothing better on earth than to hear that your father is proud of you! Imagine feeling the pride of our Father in heaven! What an incredible joy to anticipate.

> "His master said to him, 'Well done, good and faithful servant. You have been faithful over a little; I will set you over much. Enter into the joy of your master.'"[86]

Notice in this passage how Jesus says, "you have been faithful over a little." It's imperative, while we're considering the measurable nature of disciple-making that we don't put on a yoke the Lord does not assign to us. We don't want to place a one-size-fits-all expectation on the number of disciples each person makes. That can quickly become a very dangerous and easily corruptible expectation, which I don't think is Paul's heart. Some people will make thousands of disciples throughout their lives. Others will make a handful. What's important is that we are working hard to make disciples, no matter how many there are.

The mother who decides to stay home to raise and disciple her children may only have the capacity to disciple a handful of lost people she comes in contact with throughout her daily life. The full-time paid minister will obviously have many more opportunities. Both are valid and beautiful to the Lord. What matters most is not the total number of disciples we make, but that we are intentionally doing all we can to make them. The difference between making three disciples and three-thousand disciples is small. But the difference between making three disciples and zero disciples is monumental. If we are making zero disciples, we really need to evaluate our priorities before the Lord.

Jesus said, "You are My friends if you do what I command you."[87] At

---

85   1 Corinthians 3:14
86   Matthew 25:23
87   John 15:14

the end of this age, when our life's work is tested, how great will it be to know that we were a true friend to Jesus and that we did everything in our power to give Him what He wants? We will enter eternity with confidence that we obeyed His command to make disciples in every nation, and we'll remember that forever. More importantly, Jesus will remember that forever.[CITE]

Paul's fatherly guidance was not limited to Timothy's ears. It's for us. The Lord gave us an example and directives to follow:

Make many disciples.

Do the work of an evangelist.

Track your progress.

Take care of how you build.

Walk in a manner worthy of the Lord.

Work hard.

Train yourself.

Be sober-minded.

Endure suffering.

Compete by the rules; receive your crown.

You deserve your wages.

And at the end of Paul's life he said:

> "I have fought the good fight, I have finished the race, I have kept the faith. Henceforth there is laid up for me the crown of righteousness, which the Lord, the righteous judge, will award to me on that day, and not only to me but also to all who have loved His appearing."[88]

Imagine what it will be like on that Day when we look at Jesus square in the eyes and give account for the way we spent our lives, our money, our time, and our influence. Like Paul, we can say with unblushing confidence:

I obeyed the call.

---

88 2 Timothy 4:7-8

I fought the fight.

I kept the faith.

I finished the race.

I competed according to the rules.

I have received the crown of righteousness.

And not only me, but all who have loved His appearing.

> *"Think over what I say, for the Lord will give you understanding in everything."*[89]

How amazing on that day to know without a shadow of a doubt that we gave everything for that Man; that we held nothing back from Him and that we did everything in our power to give Him what He wants—and so rightfully deserves. Think of how wonderful it will be to hear that we were indeed faithful servants and stewards.

> "What then is my reward? That in my preaching I may present the gospel free of charge, so as not to make full use of my right in the gospel. For though I am free from all, I have made myself a servant to all, that I might win more of them."[90]

We will be rewarded by our King when we meet Him. One of those rewards is the ability to give Jesus His reward: people from every nation He paid for with His blood to have as an everlasting inheritance.[91]

Let's determine to build the kind of things Jesus wants and that God rewards. May we participate in bringing Him worshippers to adore Him forever in the age to come, and may we be proud of what we did on this earth so when we finally see Him face-to-face, we will hear Him say, "Well done, My good and faithful servant."

That is the ultimate reward, the "well done" of our Father in heaven.

---

89   2 Timothy 2:7
90   1 Corinthians 9:18-19
91   Ephesians 1:18

Lord, may that motivate your Bride to sing your praises with all the joy we have in You.

An Original Poem

A King prepared a banquet,
Invited all to come;
But many made excuses,
And all who came were none.
The King became upset,
They rejected His free grace;
Determined to fill His house,
Sent His servants to farthest place.
Instructed them, do more than tell;
Go to the highways and compel;
As many people as you find;
I wish to have them all as mine.
The servants so in love,
Committed take no rest;
Until the wedding hall,
Was filled with blood-bought guests.
The servants understood,
To love is to obey;
Glad to do all He asked,
To hear the Master say;
Thank you for inviting man,
Into My love and laughter;
Well done My faithful servant,
Now enter the joy of your Master.

CONCLUSION

Jesus Christ is the faithful witness.[1] He is the image of the invisible God, the exact representation of His nature.[2] The incarnate witness; the Word of God made flesh.[3] He is the ultimate demonstration of who God is to the world and to the powers and principalities of this age.[4] Jesus will personally see to it that His Great Commission is complete. He is far more committed to compelling people to come in than we are. His house will be filled whether you and I get involved or not. There will always be someone somewhere who is willing to obey Him.

But how wonderful is it that God wants us to labor alongside Him? How precious it is that the King desires to go out hand-in-hand with His servants as we invite more people to His wedding feast! What a marvelous reality that God would wrap us in His robes of righteousness and help us explain to others how they too can belong to such a good God.

> "Jesus said to His disciples, 'All authority in heaven and on earth has been given to Me. Go therefore and make disciples of all nations, baptizing them in the name of the Father and of the Son and of the Holy Spirit, teaching them

---

1 Revelation 1:5
2 Hebrews 1:3
3 John 1:14
4 Ephesians 3:10

to observe all that I have commanded you...and behold, I am with you always, to the end of the age.'"[5]

The Lord has said He will not leave us alone in the task He entrusted to us. He promised to be with us always, even to the end of the age. And He promised to send His Spirit to dwell with us and be in us forever.

"And I will ask the Father, and He will give you another Helper, to be with you forever, even the Spirit of truth, whom the world cannot receive, because it neither sees Him nor knows Him. You know Him, for He dwells with you and will be in you. I will not leave you as orphans; I will come to you."[6]

He has not left us as orphans to engage in this Great Commission alone. He will be with us always to work alongside us. He really is our Helper in this holy endeavor. He will even help us when we have failed to help Him. Remember these words from the night He was betrayed:

"Behold, the hour is coming; indeed it has come, when you will be scattered, each to his own home, and will leave Me alone. Yet I am not alone, for the Father is with Me. I have said these things to you, that in Me you may have peace. In the world you will have tribulation. But take heart; I have overcome the world."[7]

The Lord knew how His disciples would respond to His death, that they would leave Him alone and scatter back to their homes. After Jesus was crucified, His disciples were distressed and discouraged. Even His closest friends left Him and went back to fishing. But the Lord, knowing all of this beforehand, had the pastoral kindness to shepherd them through it. And He still does.

When we "leave Jesus alone" in His commission to make disciples, when we fall short of being faithful witnesses, when we fail to share His good news with our neighbors and friends, He is kind to us. We

---

5 Matthew 28:18-20
6 John 14:16-18
7 John 16:32-33

have a compassionate Father eagerly waiting to restore us. It's not too late. If you're alive, it's not too late.

King David once said:

> "Wash me thoroughly from my iniquity, and cleanse me from my sin...then I will teach transgressors your ways and sinners will return to You."[8]

I love this because when we acknowledge our shortcomings before the Lord, He will forgive us then we will announce the good news of God to the lost! His kindness to us in our failures is what leads us to repentance. And when we experience God's kindness, especially as believers, it's one of the greatest catalysts to our announcing that kindness to the wandering world around us. So, come, magnify the Lord with me, and let us exalt His name together, for the Father is seeking such people to worship Him.

Our role is simple, our task is urgent, and our King is enjoyable. I'll see you at the Marriage Supper of the Lamb. You, and all those you compelled to come with you!

Maranatha.

---

[8] Psalm 51:2,13

JORDAN SCOTT

APPENDIX A

COMPEL THEM TO COME IN

A Sermon (No. 227) Delivered on Sabbath Morning, December 5th, 1858, by the REV. C. H. Spurgeon at the Music Hall, Royal Surrey Gardens

"*Compel them to come in.*"—Luke 14:23

FEEL in such a haste to go out and obey this commandment this morning, by compelling those to come in who are now tarrying in the highways and hedges, that I cannot wait for an introduction, but must at once set about my business. Hear then, O ye that are strangers to the truth as it is in Jesus—hear then the message that I have to bring you. Ye have fallen, fallen in your father Adam; ye have fallen also in yourselves, by your daily sin and your constant iniquity; you have provoked the anger of the Most High; and as assuredly as you have sinned, so certainly must God punish you if you persevere in your iniquity, for the Lord is a God of justice, and will by no means spare the guilty. But have you not heard, hath it not long been spoken in your ears, that God, in his infinite mercy, has devised a way whereby, without any infringement upon his honour, he can have mercy upon you, the guilty and the undeserving? To you I speak; and my voice is unto you, O sons of men; Jesus Christ, very God of very God, hath descended from heaven, and was made in the likeness of sinful flesh. Begotten of the Holy Ghost, he was born of the Virgin Mary; he lived in this world a life of exemplary holiness, and of the deepest suffering, till at last he gave himself up to die for our sins, "the just for the unjust, to bring us to God." And now the plan of salvation is simply declared unto you—"Whosoever believeth in the Lord Jesus Christ shall be saved."

For you who have violated all the precepts of God, and have disdained his mercy and dared his vengeance, there is yet mercy proclaimed, for "whosoever calleth upon the name of the Lord shall be saved." "For this is a faithful saying and worthy of all acceptation, that Christ Jesus came into the world to save sinners, of whom I am chief;" "whosoever cometh unto him he will in no wise cast out, for he is able also to save unto the uttermost them that come unto God by him, seeing he ever liveth to make intercession for us." Now all that God asks of you—and this he gives you—is that you will simply look at his bleeding dying son, and trust your souls in the hands of him whose name alone can save from death and hell. Is it not a marvelous thing, that the proclamation of this gospel does not receive the unanimous consent of men? One would think that as soon as ever this was preached, "That whosoever believeth shall have eternal life," every one of you, "casting away every man his sins and his iniquities," would lay hold on Jesus Christ, and look alone to his cross. But alas! such is the desperate evil of our nature, such the pernicious depravity of our character, that this message is despised, the invitation to the gospel feast is rejected, and there are many of you who are this day enemies of God by wicked works, enemies to the God who preaches Christ to you to-day, enemies to him who sent his Son to give his life a ransom for many. Strange I say it is that it should be so, yet nevertheless it is the fact, and hence the necessity for the command of the text,—"Compel them to come in."

Children of God, ye who have believed, I shall have little or nothing to say to you this morning; I am going straight to my business—I am going after those that will not come—those that are in the byways and hedges, and God going with me, it is my duty now to fulfil this command, "Compel them to come in." First, I must, find you out; secondly, I will go to work to compel you to come in. I. First, I must FIND YOU OUT. If you read the verses that precede the text, you will find an amplification of this command: "Go out quickly into the streets and lanes of the city, and bring in hither the poor, the maimed, the halt, and the blind;" and then, afterwards, "Go out into the highways," bring in the vagrants, the highwaymen, "and into the hedges," bring in those that have no resting-place for their heads, and are lying under the hedges to rest, bring them in also, and "compel them to come in." Yes, I see you this morning, you that are poor. I am to compel you to come in. You are poor in circumstances, but this is no barrier to the kingdom of heaven, for God hath not exempted from his grace the man that shivers in rags, and who is destitute of bread. In fact, if there be any distinction made, the distinction is on your side, and for your benefit—"Unto you is the word of salvation sent"; "For the poor have the gospel preached unto them."

But especially I must speak to you who are poor, spiritually. You have no faith, you have no virtue, you have no good work, you have no grace, and what is poverty worse still, you have no hope. Ah, my Master has sent you a gracious invitation. Come and welcome to the marriage feast of his love. "Whosoever will, let him come and take of the waters of life freely." Come, I must lay hold upon you, though you be defiled with foulest filth, and though you have nought but rags upon your back, though your own righteousness has become as filthy clouts, yet must I lay hold upon you, and invite you first, and even compel you to come in. And now I see you again. You are not only poor, but you are maimed.There was a time when you thought you could work out your own salvation without God's help, when you could perform good works, attend to ceremonies, and get to heaven by yourselves; but now you are maimed, the sword of the law has cut off your hands, and now you can work no longer; you say, with bitter sorrow— "The best performance of my hands, Dares not appear before thy throne."

You have lost all power now to obey the law; you feel that when you would do good, evil is present with you. You are maimed; you have given up, as a forlorn hope, all attempt to save yourself, because you are maimed and your arms are gone. But you are worse off than that, for if you could not work your way to heaven, yet you could walk your way there along the road by faith; but you are maimed in the feet as well as in the hands; you feel that you cannot believe, that you cannot repent, that you cannot obey the stipulations of the gospel. You feel that you are utterly undone, powerless in every respect to do anything that can be pleasing to God. In fact, you are crying out— "Oh, could I but believe, Then all would easy be, I would, but cannot, Lord relieve, My help must come from thee."

To you am I sent also. Before you am I to lift up the blood-stained banner of the cross, to you am I to preach this gospel, "Whoso calleth upon the name of the Lord shall be saved;" and unto you am I to cry, "Whosoever will, let him come and take of the water of life freely." There is yet another class. You are halt. You are halting between two opinions. You are sometimes seriously inclined, and at another time worldly gaiety calls you away. What little progress you do make in religion is but a limp. You have a little strength, but that is so little that you make but painful progress. Ah, limping brother, to you also is the word of this salvation sent. Though you halt between two opinions, the Master sends me to you with this message: "How long halt ye between two opinions? if God be God, serve him; if Baal be God, serve him." Consider thy ways; set thine house in order, for thou shalt die and not live. Because I will do this, prepare to meet thy God, O Israel! Halt no longer, but decide for God and his truth.

And yet I see another class,—the blind. Yes, you that cannot see yourselves, that think yourselves good when you are full of evil, that put bitter for sweet and sweet for bitter, darkness for light and light for darkness; to you am I sent. You, blind souls that cannot see your lost estate, that do not believe that sin is so exceedingly sinful as it is, and who will not be persuaded to think that God is a just and righteous God, to you am I sent. To you too that cannot see the Saviour, that see no beauty in him that you should desire him; who see no excellence in virtue, no glories in religion, no happiness in serving God, no delight in being his children; to you, also, am I sent. Ay, to whom am I not sent if I take my text? For it goes further than this—it not only gives a particular description, so that each individual case may be met, but afterwards it makes a general sweep, and says, "Go into the highways and hedges." Here we bring in all ranks and conditions of men—my lord upon his horse in the highway, and the woman trudging about her business, the thief waylaying the traveller—all these are in the highway, and they are all to be compelled to come in, and there away in the hedges there lie some poor souls whose refuges of lies are swept away, and who are seeking not to find some little shelter for their weary heads, to you, also, are we sent this morning.

This is the universal command—compel them to come in. Now, I pause after having described the character, I pause to look at the herculean labour that lies before me. Well did Melanchthon say, "Old Adam was too strong for young Melanchthon." As well might a little child seek to compel a Samson, as I seek to lead a sinner to the cross of Christ. And yet my Master sends me about the errand. Lo, I see the great mountain before me of human depravity and stolid indifference, but by faith I cry, "Who art thou, O great mountain? before Zerubbabel thou shalt become a plain." Does my Master say, compel them to come in? Then, though the sinner be like Samson and I a child, I shall lead him with a thread. If God saith do it, if I attempt it in faith it shall be done; and if with a groaning, struggling, and weeping heart, I so seek this day to compel sinners to come to Christ, the sweet compulsions of the Holy Spirit shall go with every word, and some indeed shall be compelled to come in. II. And now to the work —directly to the work. Unconverted, unreconciled, unregenerate men and women, I am to COMPEL YOU TO COME IN. Permit me first of all to accost you in the highways of sin and tell you over again my errand.

The King of heaven this morning sends a gracious invitation to you. He says, "As I live, saith the Lord, I have no pleasure in the death of him that dieth, but had rather that he should turn unto me and live:" "Come now, and let us reason together, saith the Lord, though your sins be as scarlet they shall be as wool; though they be red like crimson they shall be whiter than snow." Dear brother, it makes my heart rejoice to think that I should have such good news to tell you, and yet I confess my soul is heavy because I see you do not think it good news, but turn away from it, and do not give it due regard. Permit me to tell you what the King has done for you. He knew your guilt, he foresaw that you would ruin yourself. He knew that his justice would demand your blood, and in order that this difficulty might be escaped, that his justice might have its full due, and that you might yet be saved, Jesus Christ hath died. Will you just for a moment glance at this picture. You see that man there on his knees in the garden of Gethsemane, sweating drops of blood. You see this next: you see that miserable sufferer tied to a pillar and lashed with terrible scourges, till the shoulder bones are seen like white islands in the midst of a sea of blood. Again you see this third picture; it is the same man hanging on the cross with hands extended, and with feet nailed fast, dying, groaning, bleeding; methought the picture spoke and said, "It is finished."

Now all this hath Jesus Christ of Nazareth done, in order that God might consistently with his justice pardon sin; and the message to you this morning is this—"Believe on the Lord Jesus Christ and thou shalt be saved." That is trust him, renounce thy works, and thy ways, and set thine heart alone on this man, who gave himself for sinners. Well brother, I have told you the message, what sayest thou unto it? Do you turn away? You tell me it is nothing to you; you cannot listen to it; that you will hear me by-and-by; but you will go your way this day and attend to your farm and merchandize. Stop brother, I was not told merely to tell you and then go about my business. No; I am told to compel you to come in; and permit me to observe to you before I further go, that there is one thing I can say—and to which God is my witness this morning, that I am in earnest with you in my desire that you should comply with this command of God. You may despise your own salvation, but I do not despise it; you may go away and forget what you shall hear, but you will please to remember that the things I now say cost me many a groan ere I came here to utter them. My inmost soul is speaking out to you, my poor brother, when I beseech you by him that liveth and was dead, and is alive for evermore, consider my master's message which he bids me now address to you.

But do you spurn it? Do you still refuse it? Then I must change my tone a minute. I will not merely tell you the message, and invite you as I do with all earnestness, and sincere affection—I will go further. Sinner, in God's name I command you to repent and believe. Do you ask me whence my authority? I am an ambassador of heaven. My credentials, some of them secret, and in my own heart; and others of them open before you this day in the seals of my ministry, sitting and standing in this hall, where God has given me many souls for my hire. As God the everlasting one hath given me a commission to preach his gospel, I command you to believe in the Lord Jesus Christ; not on my own authority, but on the authority of him who said, "Go ye into all the world and preach the gospel to every creature;" and then annexed this solemn sanction, "He that believeth and is baptized shall be saved, but he that believeth not shall be damned."

Reject my message, and remember "He that despised Moses's law, died without mercy under two or three witnesses: of how much sorer punishment, suppose ye, shall he be thought worthy, who hath trodden under foot the Son of God." An ambassador is not to stand below the man with whom he deals, for we stand higher. If the minister chooses to take his proper rank, girded with the omnipotence of God, and anointed with his holy unction, he is to command men, and speak with all authority compelling them to come in: "command, exhort, rebuke with all long-suffering." But do you turn away and say you will not be commanded? Then again will I change my note. If that avails not, all other means shall be tried. My brother, I come to you simple of speech, and I exhort you to flee to Christ. O my brother, dost thou know what a loving Christ he is? Let me tell thee from my own soul what I know of him. I, too, once despised him. He knocked at the door of my heart and I refused to open it. He came to me, times without number, morning by morning, and night by night; he checked me in my conscience and spoke to me by his Spirit, and when, at last, the thunders of the law prevailed in my conscience, I thought that Christ was cruel and unkind. O I can never forgive myself that I should have thought so ill of him.

But what a loving reception did I have when I went to him. I thought he would smite me, but his hand was not clenched in anger but opened wide in mercy. I thought full sure that his eyes would dart lightning-flashes of wrath upon me; but, instead thereof, they were full of tears. He fell upon my neck and kissed me; he took off my rags and did clothe me with his righteousness, and caused my soul to sing aloud for joy; while in the house of my heart and in the house of his church there was music and dancing, because his son that he had lost was found, and he that was dead was made alive. I exhort you, then, to look to Jesus Christ and to be lightened. Sinner, you will never regret,—I will be bondsman for my Master that you will never regret it,—you will have no sigh to go back to your state of condemnation; you shall go out of Egypt and shall go into the promised land and shall find it flowing with milk and honey. The trials of Christian life you shall find heavy, but you will find grace will make them light. And as for the joys and delights of being a child of God, if I lie this day you shall charge me with it in days to come. If you will taste and see that the Lord is good, I am not afraid but that you shall find that he is not only good, but better than human lips ever can describe.

I know not what arguments to use with you. I appeal to your own self-interests. Oh my poor friend, would it not be better for you to be reconciled to the God of heaven, than to be his enemy? What are you getting by opposing God? Are you the happier for being his enemy? Answer, pleasure-seeker; hast thou found delights in that cup? Answer me, self-righteous man: hast thou found rest for the sole of thy foot in all thy works? Oh thou that goest about to establish thine own righteousness, I charge thee let conscience speak. Hast thou found it to be a happy path? Ah, my friend, "Wherefore dost thou spend thy money for that which is not bread, and thy labour for that which satisfieth not; hearken diligently unto me, and eat ye that which is good, and let your soul delight itself in fatness." I exhort you by everything that is sacred and solemn, everything that is important and eternal, flee for your lives, look not behind you, stay not in all the plain, stay not until you have proved, and found an interest in the blood of Jesus Christ, that blood which cleanseth us from all sin.

Are you still cold and indifferent? Will not the blind man permit me to lead him to the feast? Will not my maimed brother put his hand upon my shoulder and permit me to assist him to the banquet? Will not the poor man allow me to walk side-by-side with him? Must I use some stronger words. Must I use some other compulsion to compel you to come in? Sinners, this one thing I am resolved upon this morning, if you be not saved ye shall be without excuse. Ye, from the grey-headed down to the tender age of childhood, if ye this day lay not hold on Christ, your blood shall be on your own head. If there be power in man to bring his fellow, (as there is when man is helped by the Holy Spirit) that power shall be exercised this morning, God helping me.

Come, I am not to be put off by your rebuffs; if my exhortation fails, I must come to something else. My brother, I entreat you, I entreat you stop and consider. Do you know what it is you are rejecting this morning? You are rejecting Christ, your only Saviour. "Other foundation can no man lay;" "there is none other name given among men whereby we must be saved."

My brother, I cannot bear that ye should do this, for I remember what you are forgetting: the day is coming when you will want a Saviour. It is not long ere weary months shall have ended, and your strength begin to decline; your pulse shall fail you, your strength shall depart, and you and the grim monster—death, must face each other. What will you do in the swellings of Jordan without a Saviour? Death-beds are stony things without the Lord Jesus Christ. It is an awful thing to die anyhow; he that hath the best hope, and the most triumphant faith, finds that death is not a thing to laugh at. It is a terrible thing to pass from the seen to the unseen, from the mortal to the immortal, from time to eternity, and you will find it hard to go through the iron gates of death without the sweet wings of angels to conduct you to the portals of the skies. It will be a hard thing to die without Christ. I cannot help thinking of you. I see you acting the suicide this morning, and I picture myself standing at your bedside and hearing your cries, and knowing that you are dying without hope. I cannot bear that. I think I am standing by your coffin now, and looking into your clay-cold face, and saying, "This man despised Christ and neglected the great salvation."

I think what bitter tears I shall weep then, if I think that I have been unfaithful to you, and how those eyes fast closed in death, shall seem to chide me and say, "Minister, I attended the music hall, but you were not in earnest with me; you amused me, you preached to me, but you did not plead with me. You did not know what Paul meant when he said, 'As though God did beseech you by us we pray you in Christ's stead, be ye reconciled to God.'" I entreat you let this message enter your heart for another reason. I picture myself standing at the bar of God. As the Lord liveth, the day of judgment is coming. You believe that? You are not an infidel; your conscience would not permit you to doubt the Scripture. Perhaps you may have pretended to do so, but you cannot. You feel there must be a day when God shall judge the world in righteousness. I see you standing in the midst of that throng, and the eye of God is fixed on you. It seems to you that he is not looking anywhere else, but only upon you, and he summons you before him; and he reads your sins, and he cries, "Depart ye cursed into everlasting fire in hell!"

My hearer, I cannot bear to think of you in that position; it seems as if every hair on my head must stand on end to think of any hearer of mine being damned. Will you picture yourselves in that position? The word has gone forth, "Depart, ye cursed." Do you see the pit as it opens to swallow you up? Do you listen to the shrieks and the yells of those who have preceded you to that eternal lake of torment? Instead of picturing the scene, I turn to you with the words of the inspired prophet, and I say, "Who among us shall dwell with the devouring fire? Who among us shall dwell with everlasting burnings?" Oh! my brother, I cannot let you put away religion thus; no, I think of what is to come after death. I should be destitute of all humanity if I should see a person about to poison himself, and did not dash away the cup; or if I saw another about to plunge from London Bridge, if I did not assist in preventing him from doing so; and I should be worse than a fiend if I did not now, with all love, and kindness, and earnestness, beseech you to "lay hold on eternal life," "to labour not for the meat that perisheth, but for the meat that endureth unto everlasting life."

Some hyper-calvinist would tell me I am wrong in so doing. I cannot help it. I must do it. As I must stand before my Judge at last, I feel that I shall not make full proof of my ministry unless I entreat with many tears that ye would be saved, that ye would look unto Jesus Christ and receive his glorious salvation. But does not this avail? are all our entreaties lost upon you; do you turn a deaf ear? Then again I change my note. Sinner, I have pleaded with you as a man pleadeth with his friend, and were it for my own life I could not speak more earnestly this morning than I do speak concerning yours. I did feel earnest about my own soul, but not a whit more than I do about the souls of my congregation this morning; and therefore, if ye put away these entreaties I have something else:—I must threaten you. You shall not always have such warnings as these.

A day is coming, when hushed shall be the voice of every gospel minister, at least for you; for your ear shall be cold in death. It shall not be any more threatening; it shall be the fulfillment of the threatening. There shall be no promise, no proclamations of pardon and of mercy; no peace-speaking blood, but you shall be in the land where the Sabbath is all swallowed up in everlasting nights of misery, and where the preachings of the gospel are forbidden because they would be unavailing. I charge you then, listen to this voice that now addresses your conscience; for if not, God shall speak to you in his wrath, and say unto you in his hot displeasure, "I called and ye refused; I stretched out my hand and no man regarded; therefore will I mock at your calamity; I will laugh when your fear cometh." Sinner, I threaten you again. Remember, it is but a short time you may have to hear these warnings. You imagine that your life will be long, but do you know how short it is? Have you ever tried to think how frail you are? Did you ever see a body when it has been cut in pieces by the anatomist? Did you ever see such a marvelous thing as the human frame? "Strange, a harp of a thousand strings, Should keep in tune so long."

Let but one of those cords be twisted, let but a mouthful of food go in the wrong direction, and you may die. The slightest chance, as we have it, may send you swift to death, when God wills it. Strong men have been killed by the smallest and slightest accident, and so may you. In the chapel, in the house of God, men have dropped down dead. How often do we hear of men falling in our streets—rolling out of time into eternity, by some sudden stroke. And are you sure that heart of your's is quite sound? Is the blood circulating with all accuracy? Are you quite sure of that? And if it be so, how long shall it be? O, perhaps there are some of you here that shall never see Christmas-day; it may be the mandate has gone forth already, "Set thine house in order, for thou shalt die and not live." Out of this vast congregation, I might with accuracy tell how many will be dead in a year; but certain it is that the whole of us shall never meet together again in any one assembly. Some out of this vast crowd, perhaps some two or three, shall depart ere the new year shall be ushered in. I remind you, then, my brother, that either the gate of salvation may be shut, or else you may be out of the place where the gate of mercy stands.

Come, then, let the threatening have power with you. I do not threaten because I would alarm without cause, but in hopes that a brother's threatening may drive you to the place where God hath prepared the feast of the gospel. And now, must I turn hopelessly away? Have I exhausted all that I can say? No, I will come to you again. Tell me what it is, my brother, that keeps you from Christ. I hear one say, "Oh, sir, it is because I feel myself too guilty." That cannot be, my friend, that cannot be. "But, sir, I am the chief of sinners." Friend, you are not. The chief of sinners died and went to heaven many years ago; his name was Saul of Tarsus, afterwards called Paul the apostle. He was the chief of sinners, I know he spoke the truth. "No," but you say still, "I am too vile." You cannot be viler than the chief of sinners. You must, at least, be second worst. Even supposing you are the worst now alive, you are second worst, for he was chief. But suppose you are the worst, is not that the very reason why you should come to Christ. The worse a man is, the more reason he should go to the hospital or physician. The more poor you are, the more reason you should accept the charity of another. Now, Christ does not want any merits of your's. He gives freely. The worse you are, the more welcome you are.

But let me ask you a question: Do you think you will ever get better by stopping away from Christ? If so, you know very little as yet of the way of salvation at all. No, sir, the longer you stay, the worse you will grow; your hope will grow weaker, your despair will become stronger; the nail with which Satan has fastened you down will be more firmly clenched, and you will be less hopeful than ever. Come, I beseech you, recollect there is nothing to be gained by delay, but by delay everything may be lost. "But," cries another, "I feel I cannot believe." No, my friend, and you never will believe if you look first at your believing. Remember, I am not come to invite you to faith, but am come to invite you to Christ. But you say, "What is the difference?" Why, just this, if you first of all say, "I want to believe a thing," you never do it. But your first inquiry must be, "What is this thing that I am to believe?" Then will faith come as the consequence of that search. Our first business has not to do with faith, but with Christ. Come, I beseech you, on Calvary's mount, and see the cross. Behold the Son of God, he who made the heavens and the earth, dying for your sins.

Look to him, is there not power in him to save? Look at his face so full of pity. Is there not love in his heart to prove him willing to save? Sure sinner, the sight of Christ will help thee to believe. Do not believe first, and then go to Christ, or else thy faith will be a worthless thing; go to Christ without any faith, and cast thyself upon him, sink or swim. But I hear another cry, "Oh sir, you do not know how often I have been invited, how long I have rejected the Lord." I do not know, and I do not want to know; all I know is that my Master has sent me, to compel you to come in; so come along with you now. You may have rejected a thousand invitations; don't make this the thousandth-and-one. You have been up to the house of God, and you have only been gospel hardened. But do I not see a tear in your eye; come, my brother, don't be hardened by this morning's sermon. O, Spirit of the living God, come and melt this heart for it has never been melted, and compel him to come in! I cannot let you go on such idle excuses as that; if you have lived so many years slighting Christ, there are so many reasons why now you should not slight him. But did I hear you whisper that this was not a convenient time? Then what must I say to you? When will that convenient time come? Shall it come when you are in hell? Will that time be convenient? Shall it come when you are on your dying bed, and the death throttle is in your throat—shall it come then? Or when the burning sweat is scalding your brow; and then again, when the cold clammy sweat is there, shall those be convenient times? When pains are racking you, and you are on the borders of the tomb?

No, sir, this morning is the convenient time. May God make it so. Remember, I have no authority to ask you to come to Christ to-morrow. The Master has given you no invitation to come to him next Tuesday. The invitation is, "To-day if ye will hear his voice, harden not your hearts as in the provocation," for the Spirit saith "to-day." "Come now and let us reason together;" why should you put it off? It may be the last warning you shall ever have. Put it off, and you may never weep again in chapel. You may never have so earnest a discourse addressed to you. You may not be pleaded with as I would plead with you now. You may go away, and God may say, "He is given unto idols, let him alone." He shall throw the reins upon your neck; and then, mark—your course is sure, but it is sure damnation and swift destruction. And now again, is it all in vain? Will you not now come to Christ? Then what more can I do? I have but one more resort, and that shall be tried. I can be permitted to weep for you; I can be allowed to pray for you. You shall scorn the address if you like; you shall laugh at the preacher; you shall call him fanatic if you will; he will not chide you, he will bring no accusation against you to the great Judge.

Your offence, so far as he is concerned, is forgiven before it is committed; but you will remember that the message that you are rejecting this morning is a message from one who loves you, and it is given to you also by the lips of one who loves you. You will recollect that you may play your soul away with the devil, that you may listlessly think it a matter of no importance; but there lives at least one who is in earnest about your soul, and one who before he came here wrestled with his God for strength to preach to you, and who when he has gone from this place will not forget his hearers of this morning. I say again, when words fail us we can give tears—for words and tears are the arms with which gospel ministers compel men to come in. You do not know, and I suppose could not believe, how anxious a man whom God has called to the ministry feels about his congregation, and especially about some of them. I heard but the other day of a young man who attended here a long time, and his father's hope was that he would be brought to Christ.

He became acquainted, however, with an infidel; and now he neglects his business, and lives in a daily course of sin. I saw his father's poor wan face; I did not ask him to tell me the story himself, for I felt it was raking up a trouble and opening a sore; I fear, sometimes, that good man's grey hairs may be brought with sorrow to the grave. Young men, you do not pray for yourselves, but your mothers wrestle for you. You will not think of your own souls, but your fathers anxiety is exercised for you. I have been at prayer meetings, when I have heard children of God pray there, and they could not have prayed with more earnestness and more intensity of anguish if they had been each of them seeking their own soul's salvation. And is it not strange that we should be ready to move heaven and earth for your salvation, and that still you should have no thought for yourselves, no regard to eternal things? Now I turn for one moment to some here. There are some of you here members of Christian churches, who make a profession of religion, but unless I be mistaken in you—and I shall be happy if I am—your profession is a lie. You do not live up to it, you dishonour it; you can live in the perpetual practice of absenting yourselves from God's house, if not in sins worse than that.

Now I ask such of you who do not adorn the doctrine of God your Saviour, do you imagine that you can call me your pastor, and yet that my soul cannot tremble over you and in secret weep for you? Again, I say it may be but little concern to you how you defile the garments of your Christianity, but it is a great concern to God's hidden ones, who sigh and cry, and groan for the iniquities of the professors of Zion. Now does anything else remain to the minister besides weeping and prayer? Yes, there is one thing else. God has given to his servants not the power of regeneration, but he has given them something akin to it. It is impossible for any man to regenerate his neighbour; and yet how are men born to God? Does not the apostle say of such an one that he was begotten by him in his bonds. Now the minister has a power given him of God, to be considered both the father and the mother of those born to God, for the apostle said he travailed in birth for souls till Christ was formed in them. What can we do then? We can now appeal to the Spirit.

I know I have preached the gospel, that I have preached it earnestly; I challenge my Master to honour his own promise. He has said it shall not return unto me void, and it shall not. It is in his hands, not mine. I cannot compel you, but thou O Spirit of God who hast the key of the heart, thou canst compel. Did you ever notice in that chapter of the Revelation, where it says, "Behold I stand at the door and knock," a few verses before, the same person is described, as he who hath the key of David. So that if knocking will not avail, he has the key and can and will come in. Now if the knocking of an earnest minister prevail not with you this morning, there remains still that secret opening of the heart by the Spirit, so that you shall be compelled. I thought it my duty to labour with you as though I must do it; now I throw it into my Master's hands. It cannot be his will that we should travail in birth, and yet not bring forth spiritual children. It is with him; he is master of the heart, and the day shall declare it, that some of you constrained by sovereign grace have become the willing captives of the all-conquering Jesus, and have bowed your hearts to him through the sermon of this morning.

JORDAN SCOTT

APPENDIX B

A FULL & FAITHFUL WITNESS

Chapter one briefly touched on what a person needs to hear to call on the Lord for salvation. Here I have unpacked these vital elements in a little more detail, with Scripture citations.

MAN HAS INHERITED A CORRUPTED NATURE AND WILL BE JUDGED ETERNALLY

We need to look no further for the necessity of a Savior than the fact that one was provided. Every human heart is desperately sick and deceitful above all things.[1] We are all born deserving the wrath of God.[2] We have inherited guilt[3] and contribute to it every day we live. Man is entirely unable to rescue himself from sin or its consequences. If we say we have no sin, we deceive ourselves.[4] And not only are we guilty *because* we sin[5] but because we *are* sin. Jesus had to "become

---
1 Jeremiah 17:9
2 John 3:36; Romans 3:23; Ephesians 2:1-3
3 1 Corinthians 15:22
4 1 John 1:8
5 Romans 3:10-20

sin" for our sake so that we could become the righteousness of God.[6] I reject the well-intended phrase, "God loves the sinner but hates the sin." Yes, God loved us first, while we were sinners,[7] but God hates the wicked[8] and is angry with them every day.[9] Sin is not punished separately from the sinner. Remember, it is the sinner who is in Hell, not just his sin.[10] If God said we need saving, then we need saving. "And there is salvation in no one else, for there is no other name under heaven given among men by which we must be saved."[11]

JESUS IS GOD IN THE FLESH, BORN OF A VIRGIN AND WITHOUT SIN

Jesus has always been God from the beginning.[12] Christ is the image of the invisible God, (Colossians 1:15), the fullness of Deity dwelling bodily.[13] All things were made by Him, and through Him and for Him, and in Him, all things hold together.[14] He was manifested in the likeness of human flesh.[15] As a newborn infant, Jesus is called Mighty God and Everlasting Father.[16] There is no question in the Jewish mind when Jesus says; "Before Abraham was, I AM," that He is announcing Himself as Yahweh.[17] Jesus proves His Deity by healing a paralyzed man, showing that He has the authority to forgive sins, something only God can do![18] We celebrate the humility of God to clothe Himself in our form. Yahweh, the God of Abraham, Isaac, and Jacob, condescended to His people, stooped low to become like us. He came down from His throne to be with His creation, in the very form of His creation, when the Holy Spirit of God overshadowed a virgin girl from Israel.[19] Jesus is entirely God and fully man.[20] He is

---

6   2 Corinthians 5:21
7   Romans 5:6-10
8   Psalm 11:5
9   Psalm 7:11-12
10 Luke 12:4-5
11 Acts 4:12
12 John 1:1-3; 10:27-30; Philippians 2:5; Revelation 3:14
13 Colossians 1:15,18-19; 2:8-9
14 Colossians 1:16; Hebrews 1:2
15 Romans 8:3; Philippians 2:6; Hebrews 1:1-13
16 Isaiah 9:6-7
17 John 8:58-59; 5:18-27
18 Mark 2:1-12
19 Luke 1:34-35
20 Hebrews 2:14-17

not half-God and half-man like Hercules; God had sex with no one. The Lord is fully God contained in a fully human frame. He is God and person—the man Christ Jesus.[21] This is no Greek myth; this is Hebrew history! Jesus is perfect and walked the earth entirely without sin; He is the lamb without defect.[22]

GOD RESCUED MAN FROM WRATH BY PUNISHING HIS INNOCENT SON IN THEIR PLACE

Jesus was crucified for man in the place of those who will have him. He died the death you deserve; He took the punishment you earned. Jesus bore our grief and was pierced for our transgressions. He was smitten by God and afflicted. And the Lord has laid on Him the iniquity of us all. He was judged for our sins in our place, and the Lord was pleased to crush Him. Jesus rendered Himself as a guilt offering, which God will see and be satisfied. He bore the sin of many and poured himself out to death.[23] A bloody, violent, wrath-satisfying crushing of Christ took place for us to be made right with God. He was forsaken, stricken, and cursed.[24] He was beaten, mocked, scourged, and humiliated by men.[25] He was betrayed and denied by his closest friends.[26] He was given over to bloodthirsty men who cursed their own children to crucify Him.[27] Jesus drank the cup His Father poured for Him in the garden.[28] That cup of horror and desolation mixed to full strength,[29] that cup of staggering meant for the nations,[30] Jesus swallowed on our behalf. And if He didn't, you would have had to take it yourself. If Jesus were in agony, sweating blood at the thought of drinking it,[31] you would not have been able to bear it. Let it be known, God crushed his own Son. It was not merely the hands of men. Sin did not surprise God. The Cross was not a backup plan, it was the only plan, and it was premeditated. "This

---

21 1 Timothy 2:5
22 Isaiah 53:9; Hebrews 4:15; 1 Peter 1:18-19; 2:22; 1 John 3:5
23 Paraphrased from Isaiah 53
24 Matthew 27:46; Romans 3:21-28; Galatians 3:13
25 Matthew 27:26-30
26 Matthew 26; Mark 14; Luke 22; John 18
27 Matthew 27:22-25
28 Luke 22:42
29 Ezekiel 23:31-34
30 Isaiah 51:17; Zechariah 12:2
31 Luke 22:39-44

Jesus delivered up according to the definite plan and foreknowledge of God, you crucified and killed by the hands of lawless men."[32]

JESUS WAS RESURRECTED FROM DEATH AND ASCENDED INTO HEAVEN UNTIL HIS RETURN

Our pardon was ordered by God, signed with blood, and proven to be an acceptable offering by His resurrection. Jesus did not stay dead. He was resurrected per the Scriptures[33] and is Himself the resurrection.[34] God brought Jesus back to life after being buried in a tomb for three days,[35] attesting before men to the divinity of Christ[36] and affirming all Jesus said in His time on earth, including His claims to be God.[37] Afterward, He appeared to women at His tomb,[38] to men walking to Emmaus,[39] spent forty days with His disciples,[40] then appeared to over five hundred men at one time.[41] We base this historical event, like all history, on the eyewitness accounts of trustworthy men who were there to testify—even unto death—that what they saw was real. Men who touched the holes in Jesus' body that still bore scars from His sacrifice[42] and then bowed down to worship Him (and were not corrected). Jesus' closest friends stood with mouths agape staring onto the sky as He ascended into the heavens.[43] Whether He flew like Superman or floated like the Lorax, I don't know. Stephen testifies later that He saw Jesus sitting at the right hand of God[44] as our High Priest[45] and Advocate,[46] forever making intercession for us.[47] To the disciples gazing into the sky, two men said to them, "Men of Galilee, why do you stand looking into Heaven? This Jesus, who

---

32 Acts 2:23
33 Matthew 26:2; Acts 2:24
34 John 11:25
35 1 Corinthians 15:3
36 Acts 2:22; 13:30-31; 17:31
37 Acts 3:13-15
38 John 20:11-18
39 Luke 24:13-15
40 Acts 1:1-3
41 1 Corinthians 15:3-8
42 John 20:27-29
43 Mark 16:19; Acts 1:9-10; Ephesians 4:8-10
44 Acts 7:56
45 Hebrews 4:14-16; chapters 7-8.
46 1 John 2:1-2
47 Isaiah 53:12; Hebrews 7:25

was taken up from you into Heaven, will come in the same way as you saw Him go into Heaven."[48]

"And if Christ has not been raised, then our preaching is in vain, and your faith is in vain. We are even found to be misrepresenting God because we testified about God that He raised Christ, whom he did not raise if it is true that the dead are not raised...and if Christ has not been raised, your faith is futile, and you are still in your sins...if in Christ we have hope in this life only, we are of all people most to be pitied."[49]

EVERY PERSON IS RESPONSIBLE FOR REPENTING FROM SIN AND TURNING TOWARD CHRIST

All throughout Scripture, we're told to repent.[50] God's patience is intended to lead us to repentance, but if we do not repent, we will be judged.[51] The day is coming when the thoughts and intentions of every person's desperately sick heart will be laid bare, naked and exposed before the eyes of whom we all must give account.[52] Nothing will be kept from His knowledge, nothing is hidden that will not be revealed.[53] If a person does not repent, God's wrath will not be lifted from them. "Whoever believes in the Son has eternal life; whoever does not obey the Son shall not see life, but the wrath of God remains on him."[54]

---

48 Acts 1:11
49 1 Corinthians 15:14-19
50 Isaiah 30:15; Matthew 4:17; Mark 1:14-15; Acts 3:19; 17:30-31
51 Romans 2:4-5
52 Hebrews 4:12-13
53 Matthew 10:26; Luke 8:17; 12:2
54 John 3:36

JORDAN SCOTT

APPENDIX C

THE MIGHTY HAND OF SAVING GRACE

In the first chapter, I briefly mentioned how a person comes to saving faith in Jesus. Here I have elaborated more and provided Scripture references.

YOU WERE KNOWN BEFORE YOU WERE MADE AND WERE PREDESTINED FOR ADOPTION AS A SON

Why do I say "predestined"? Because Romans 8:28-30, Ephesians 1:4-5, and Revelation 13:8 say it. God is not interested in sharing the glory for His work with anyone else.[1] If your dad gave you a present you didn't deserve, just because he wanted to, but you told your friends that you earned it by working, you would be a liar. God is not unclear about his free gift of salvation, and we shouldn't be either. Every man and woman who right now belongs to Christ has come the same way, by grace through faith without the ability to boast in their contribution.[2]

It's crucial that we understand God's predestining has no bearing on

---

[1] Isaiah 43:11; 44:24; Ephesians 2:9
[2] Ephesians 2:8-9

who we decide to share the Gospel with. No man can know which unbeliever has been predestined and which one has not. It would be sinfully presumptuous to make a claim like that. God alone knows who will and who will not come to him. Speculations about who is "elect" that would prevent us from preaching the Gospel are far from the character of God and even farther from sense and reason. Our job is to scatter seed (like the sower of Matthew 13) and let the Word of God fall where it may.

THE FATHER DRAWS YOU TO JESUS

You have been chosen out of the world.[3] This fact is quite inarguable when Jesus says that no one comes to Him unless the Father draws Him.[4] God, who said let the light shine out of darkness, has shone into your heart to give light to the knowledge of the glory of God in the face of Jesus Christ.[5] You are no longer blind and perishing.[6] God has unveiled the beauty of His Son to you and removed your blindness. He showed Himself to you, and you suddenly found Him beautiful when you didn't see only moments before. That is His work, His doing; His grand accomplishment to cause you to adore Him, not by some external force, but by causing you to want Him yourself.

HIS KINDNESS SHOULD BRING YOU TO REPENTANCE[7]

Here is the first time in the whole act of salvation that you have a part to play. You are responsible to God for how you respond. But when you look at the options, is there really a choice to be made? Either Christ takes your punishment, or you do; what option do you have? To say, "No, thank you, Savior?"

Believe and be baptized. If you now believe, you should get baptized. Why? Because the Baptists said, you should? No, because your Bible did.[8] Obedience to Christ is the leading indicator of your love for Him. If you say you love Jesus but don't obey the things He says, you may have reason to question your love for Jesus. Do I believe that

---

[3] Matthew 11:27; John 16:16,19
[4] John 6:44
[5] 2 Corinthians 4:6
[6] 2 Corinthians 4:3-5
[7] Acts 2:37-38; 2 Corinthians 7:9-10; Romans 2:4; 2 Timothy 2:24-26
[8] Acts 2:38-39

baptism is essential for salvation? No. Do I believe men who have been saved should do it? Yes.[9]

You are a new creature

If you hate the sin you once loved,[10] it is because you are a new creature.[11] You have been born again.[12] We have been given a new heart[13] and new affections. God now dwells in you by His Spirit.[14] We are sealed by the Holy Spirit, the guarantee of our inheritance in God until we acquire possession of it.[15]

---

9   Romans 6:2-4; 1 Peter 3:20-21
10 Romans 7:15-8:1
11 2 Corinthians 5:17
12 John 3:3-8; Titus 3:4-7
13 Ezekiel 36:22-27
14 Romans 8:9-11; 1 Corinthians 3:16
15 Ephesians 1:13-14

ACKNOWLEDGMENTS

"Thanks be to God, who in Christ always leads us in triumphal procession, and through us spreads the fragrance of the knowledge of Him everywhere."
2 Corinthians 2:14

Dalton and Anna, without you, I might still be a hotel bellhop. Thank you both for your persistent friendship.

JORDAN SCOTT

ABOUT THE AUTHOR

After coming to faith in Jesus as a young man living in New Zealand, Jordan Scott moved to the Middle East to serve unreached and unengaged people groups with a witness of the Gospel. He gives leadership to addiction recovery programs in the Turkish world, where he lives with his wife and children. Jordan is the host of The Way podcast available in the FAI app.

ABOUT FAI

Frontier Alliance International is an organization committed to Romans 15:20 and devoted to exalting the worth of Jesus Christ among the unreached and unengaged at the end of the age. For more information on our relief, training, film, publishing, and other initiatives, visit faimission.org. Download the FAI app for free access to our original films, TV shows, podcasts, breaking news alerts from the 10/40 Window, Bible study resources, and more.

Because life is a vapor. Because death is gain. Because obedience. Because "do not take My Name in vain." Because life is Christ. Because faith. Because Gospel. Because it's for His glory's sake. Because the King will return. Because "the greatest of these is love." Because Psalm seventy-two. Because Revelation twenty-one. Because hope. Because this story isn't done. Because we're going to make plowshares out of all our swords and every gun. Because barrel bombs shouldn't fall. Because He took on flesh and blood. Because He said "go tell them all." Because He still does. Because nothing matters more than this. Because every nation needs a witness. Because the unreached deserve it. Because so many haven't heard yet. Because the manger. Because He knelt to wash our feet. Because grace. Because His blood still intercedes. Because the prophecies. Because Jerusalem and "blessed is He." Because it's not because He needs us. Because Zion.

because Jesus.

Made in United States
North Haven, CT
28 February 2023

A Call To Compel

The Simplicity, Urgency, and Joy of Making Disciples

JORDAN SCOTT